T0036130

EYEWITNESS

BIRD

Pheasant wing
Crow egg
Guillemot egg
Magpie egg
Wagtail nest
Mallard wing
Peacock tail covert

EYEWITNESS

BIRD

Written by

DAVID BURNIE

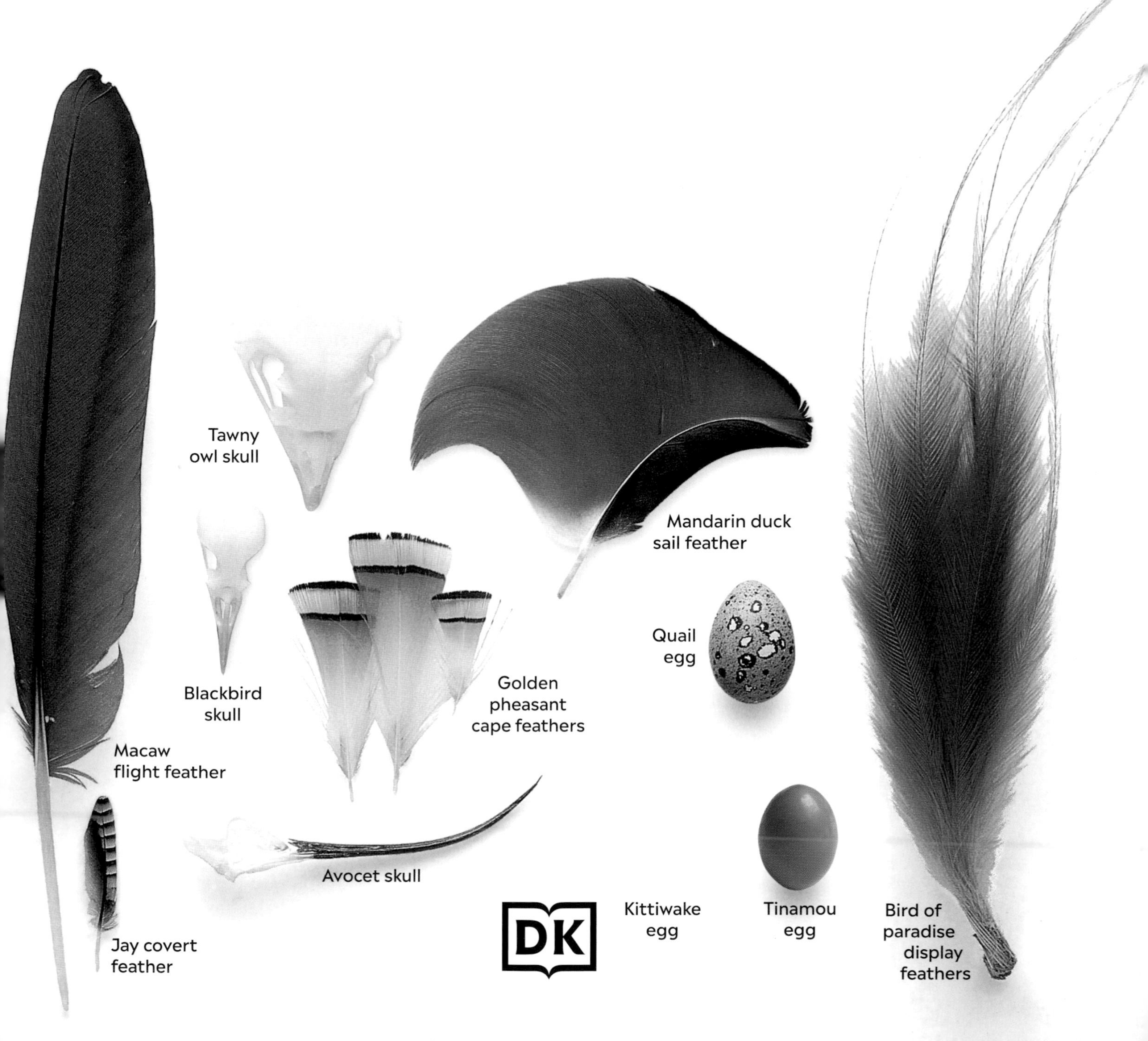

Green woodpecker wing

Partridge egg

REVISED EDITION

DK DELHI

Deputy Managing Editor Sreshtha Bhattacharya
Senior Art Editor Vikas Chauhan
Assistant Art Editor Prateek Maurya
Senior Picture Researcher Sumedha Chopra
Managing Editor Kingshuk Ghoshal
Managing Art Editor Govind Mittal
DTP Designers Vikram Singh, Deepak Mittal
DTP Coordinators Jagtar Singh, Vishal Bhatia
Production Editor Pawan Kumar
Project Jacket Art Editor Juhi Sheth
Jacket Designer Vidushi Chaudhry
Senior Jackets Coordinator Priyanka Sharma Saddi

DK LONDON

Senior Editor Michelle Crane
Senior Art Editor Sheila Collins
US Editor Heather Wilcox
US Executive Editor Lori Cates Hand
Managing Editor Francesca Baines
Managing Art Editor Philip Letsu
Production Controller Jack Matts
Senior Jackets Designer Surabhi Wadhwa-Gandhi
Jacket Design Development Manager Sophia MTT
Publisher Andrew Macintyre
Associate Publishing Director Liz Wheeler
Art Director Karen Self
Publishing Director Jonathan Metcalf

Consultant Jamie Dunning

FIRST EDITION

Project Editor Janice Lacock
Art Editor Carole Ash
Managing Art Editor Jane Owen
Special Photography Peter Chadwick and Kim Taylor
Editorial consultants The staff of the Natural History Museum, London, UK

This Eyewitness ® Guide has been conceived by Dorling Kindersley Limited and Editions Gallimard

This American Edition, 2024
First American Edition, 1988
Published in the United States by DK Publishing
1745 Broadway, 20th Floor, New York, NY 10019

24 25 26 27 28 10 9 8 7 6 5 4 3 2 1
001-338861-Apr/2024

Published in Great Britain by Dorling Kindersley Limited

A catalog record for this book is available from the Library of Congress
ISBN 978-0-7440-9210-3 (Paperback)
ISBN 978-0-7440-9211-0 (ALB)

DK books are available at special discounts when purchased in bulk for sales promotions, premiums, fund-raising, or educational use. For details, contact: DK Publishing Special Markets, 1745 Broadway, 20th Floor, New York, NY 10019
SpecialSales@dk.com

Printed and bound in China

www.dk.com

Curlew feather

Wild turkey feather

Pheasant feather

Flamingo feather

Robin egg

Razorbill egg

Parrot skull

This book was made with Forest Stewardship Council™ certified paper—one small step in DK's commitment to a sustainable future.
Learn more at
www.dk.com/uk/information/sustainability

Contents

Budgerigar feather
Rock pebbler feather
Cockatiel feather

Remember

Never touch birds' eggs in the wild, and keep your distance from nesting birds.

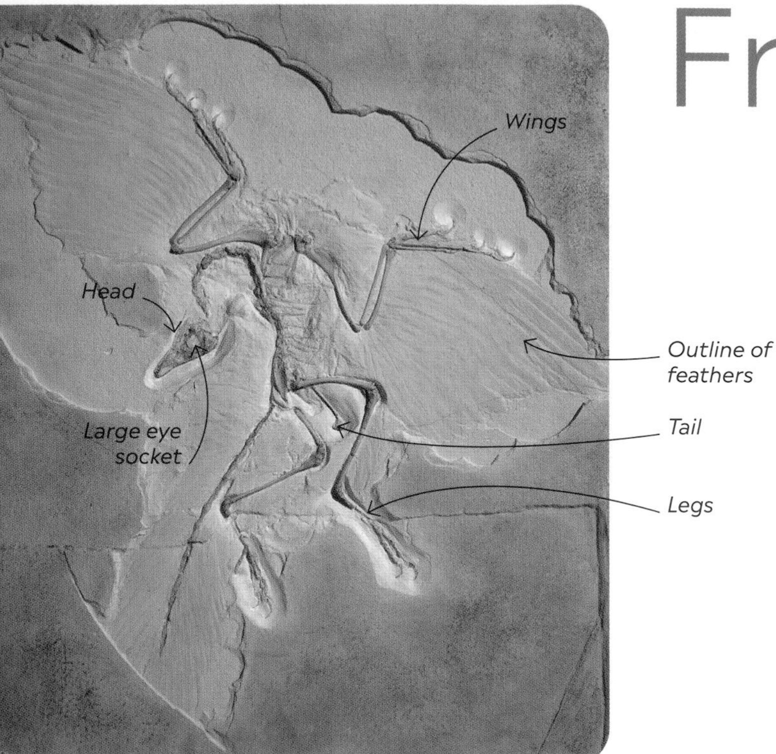

From dinosaur **to bird**

In 1861, quarry workers in Germany discovered the fossil of *Archaeopteryx*, a creature with feathers, a bony tail, clawed wings, and dinosaur-like teeth. The fossil provided strong evidence that birds evolved from dinosaurs more than 150 million years ago. Today, almost 11,000 species of birds are found in all major habitats of the world.

Feathered dinosaur

Since the 1860s, 11 different fossils of *Archaeopteryx* have been found in Germany. The "Berlin *Archaeopteryx*" (above) was discovered in the 1870s. Its wings and legs are well preserved, as are the outlines of its feathers.

Front view of a crow's skeleton

Skull

Neck

Backbone

Leg bone

Staying balanced

Birds are compact creatures. A bird's heavy wing and leg muscles are packed around the ribcage and backbone. This allows a bird to stay balanced both in the sky and on the ground.

Many pterosaurs had head crests.

Pterosaur

Prehistoric reptiles called pterosaurs had leathery wings made of skin, but were unrelated to birds. They died out at the same time as the dinosaurs, about 66 million years ago.

The slender wings were used for soaring over the ocean.

As dead as the dodo

The dodo, shown here in an illustration from Lewis Carroll's *Alice's Adventures in Wonderland*, was one of many birds driven to extinction by human action. The dodo was a flightless bird found in Madagascar and other islands in the Indian Ocean. It became extinct in the late 17th century.

Streamlined body

Although they differ in size, flying birds like the crow all have a very similar overall shape. This is because they need to be streamlined and cannot afford structures that would make them weigh more.

The bird skeleton

The most prominent feature of the skeletons of flying birds is the keel—a projection from the breastbone that anchors the wing muscles. The forelimbs are adapted for flight, while the beak (or bill) is used for feeding and preening.

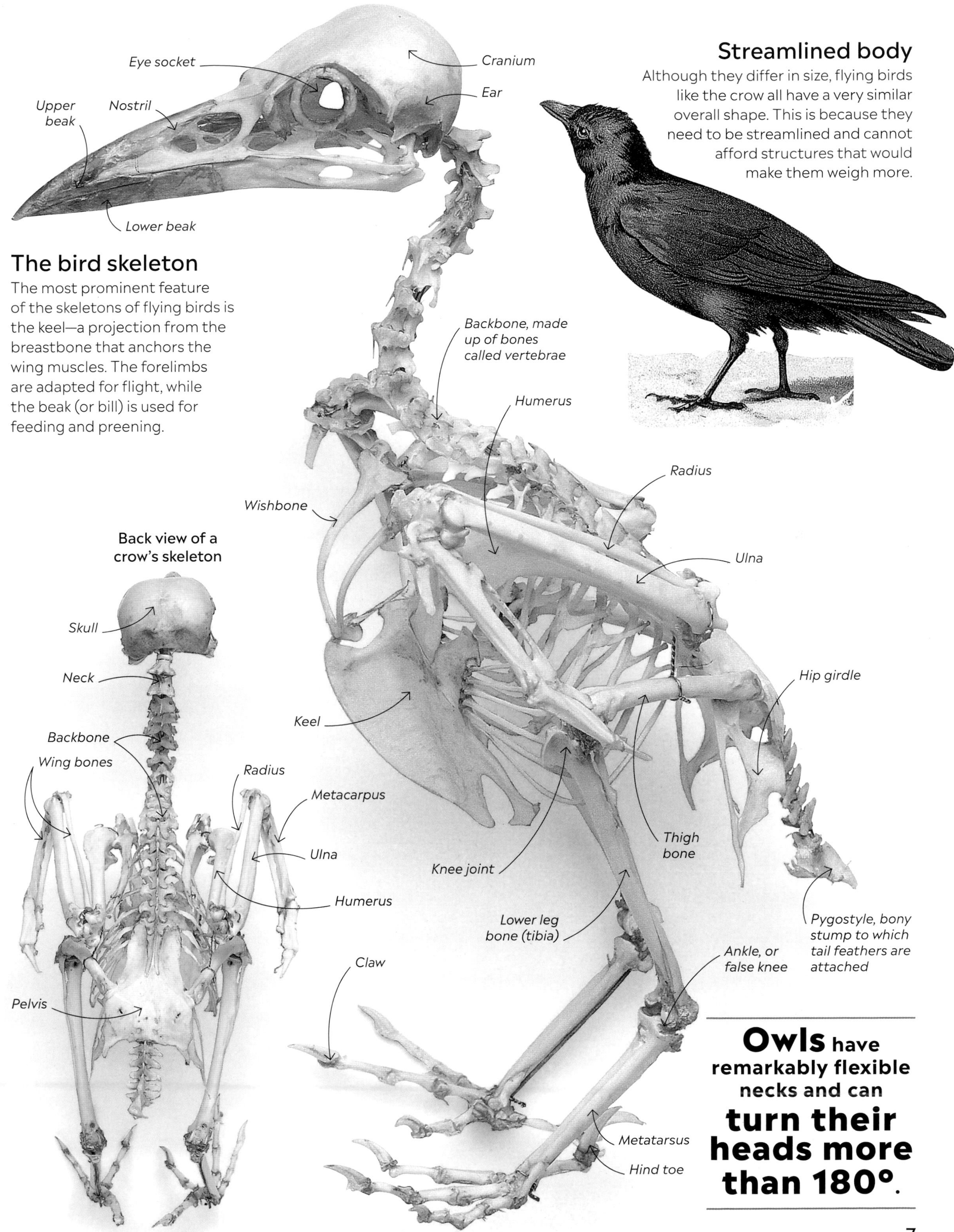

Owls have remarkably flexible necks and can **turn their heads more than 180°.**

Anatomy

Birds come in a wide range of sizes, from the smallest, the bee hummingbird, to the largest, the North African ostrich. The enormous variety of species can be found in habitats as diverse as polar regions and tropical rain forests.

Ear coverts
Beak
Mantle
Eye
Secondary flight feathers
Primary flight feathers
Breast
Flank
Toe
Tail

Outer surface

A bird's entire body, except its bill and feet, is usually covered with feathers. Some birds, such as vultures, have bare heads and necks.

Cross-section of a bird's bone

Saving weight

Birds need a lightweight skeleton to be able to fly. Unlike the bones of land animals, the long bones of flying birds are hollow and are reinforced with lightweight internal struts. In many flightless and diving birds, however, the bones are solid.

Digestive system

Birds have no teeth, so their digestive system has to carry out all the stages of food breakdown. The lower part of the stomach, known as the gizzard, grinds the food into a pulp.

Gullet
Stomach
Small intestine
Crop
Liver
Gizzard
Rectum

Birds have high body temperatures, which can go up to 110°F (43.5°C).

Design for flight

Flight makes enormous demands on a bird's body. Once airborne, a bird like a heron may save energy by gliding, but it requires all the power it can produce for its initial takeoff. As well as having a lightweight skeleton, birds have a high metabolic rate—the speed at which they turn food into energy, which helps them fly.

Long neck

Birds have more bones in the neck than most vertebrate animals. A bird such as a heron has a flexible neck, which it uses to catch food and to preen all parts of its body with its beak.

Animals that fly

Birds and bats are the only vertebrate animals capable of true powered flight. Some other animals are able to glide on unpowered "wings."

Flying frogs
The webbing between the frog's feet act like miniature parachutes to enable it to glide between trees.

Flying squirrels
Some squirrels use loose flaps of skin to glide through the air.

Flying fish
The gurnard can glide above the water on extended fins.

The wing

Birds are the fastest and most powerful fliers in the animal kingdom. A bird's wing is light, strong, and flexible. It is also convex in shape, curving slightly from front to back, which helps pull the bird upward as it flaps through the air. Although the size and shape of wings vary, they all share the same basic design.

Within the limit

A bird's wings can bear its weight, plus anything it is carrying, such as food or nesting materials.

Bald eagle carrying a mallard

Icarus falling to the ground

Too high

In Greek legend, Icarus flew too close to the sun, causing the wax that held his feathers to melt. But birds flying at high altitude have to deal with quite different and much more real problems—little oxygen and intense cold.

Alula

This group of feathers from an owl covers the front edge of the wing. The alula provides lift to the wing during unsteady maneuvers, such as landing.

Flapping failures

Early inventors did not realize that flapping flight would always be beyond the power of human muscles.

The Flying Philosopher *etching*

Primary flight feathers

The "primaries" produce the power for flight. The outermost primary feathers can be used for steering.

EYEWITNESS

Leonardo da Vinci

Italian artist Leonardo da Vinci (1452–1519) was also a brilliant engineer. He was fascinated by how birds fly. He studied their wing structures and observed their flight. These observations inspired him to design many flying machines, but none of them took off.

A bird's plumage weighs more than its skeleton.

First finger *Wrist bones* *Thumb*

Second finger

Wing bones

The wing bones form a system of lightweight levers for the wing muscles to act on.

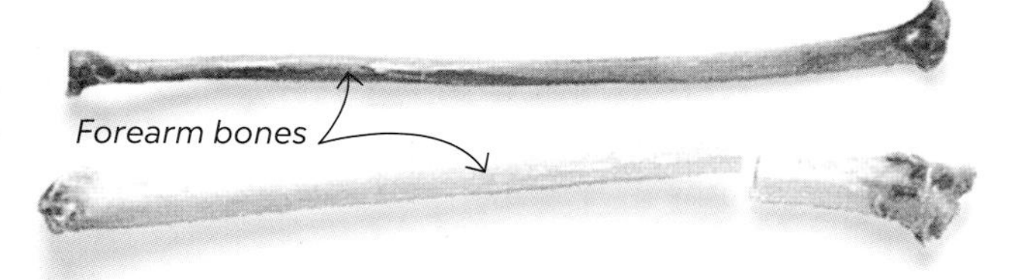

Part of the upper arm bone

Lesser coverts

These shape the part of the wing that meets the oncoming air.

Main coverts

Covert feathers protect the flight feathers below.

Secondary flight feathers

The "secondaries" add to the curve that provides lift.

Tertiary flight feathers

These innermost flight feathers shape the wing into the body to prevent turbulence during flight.

Wings and arms

Bird wings and human arms have evolved from the same type of limb.

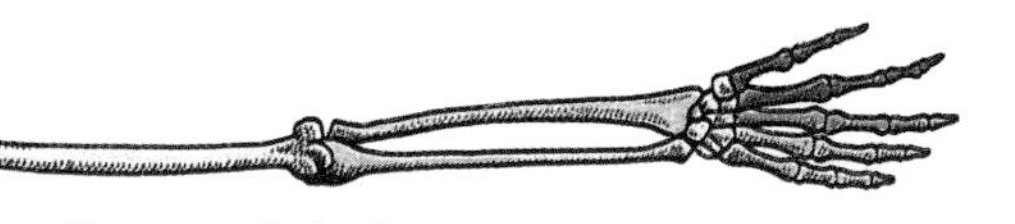

Bones of the human arm

Bones of the bird's wing

Maneuverability

Many birds have broad, rounded wings that help them steer and accelerate. This type of wing is common in birds that live on the ground and woodland birds that must avoid trees in flight.

Owl flight

The barn owl has a slow, buoyant flight.

Finch flight

Finches bounce up and down and usually fly above treetop level.

Greenfinch wing

Quick turn

The greenfinch has a blunt, rounded wing shape that allows it to turn quickly in the air.

Greenfinches

Primary flight feathers

Fringed feather edges reduce air turbulence.

Soft, downy wing coverts

Barn owl wing

Barn owl

Muffled wings

Fringed feathers muffle the sound of the owl's wings so it can sneak up on its prey.

Broad flight feathers

Rollers

Perch to perch

The roller catches small animals by swooping down on them from its perches on walls and trees.

Light and dark barring

Broad wing surface for maneuverability

Crested pigeon wing

Roller flight

The roller has a heavy up-and-down flight.

Roller wing

Quick escape

Doves and pigeons have strong wing muscles for fast takeoff and acceleration up to 50 mph (80 kmph).

Turtle dove

Green woodpecker wing

Green coloring for camouflage

Woodpecker flight

Woodpeckers climb and dive much more steeply than most other birds.

Pheasants in flight

Up-and-down flight

A green woodpecker spends a lot of time on the ground and flies very short distances. It has shorter, rounded wings.

Green woodpecker

Pheasant wing

Folded flight feathers

Camouflaged inner feathers conceal bird on ground.

Vertical takeoff

If alarmed, pheasants take off almost vertically on their broad wings.

Flying for protection

Pheasants and grouse spend most of their time on the ground. On sensing danger, they crouch down, then bring their opened wings sharply downward to burst into the air.

Pheasant flight

Rapid wing beats are followed by a long glide.

Female black grouse wing

Female black grouse

Male black grouse wing

Long flight feathers for short gliding flights

Speed and **endurance**

Birds such as swifts can fly nonstop for up to ten months, as their wings are adapted for continuous use. In a similar way, the wings of all other birds have evolved for a particular kind of flight. Birds with pointed wings fly rapidly and powerfully. This wing shape provides the bird with enough lift, without producing too much drag.

Fearful hunter

The peregrine falcon is one of the world's fastest birds. It can dive at up to 175 mph (280 kmph) in pursuit of prey. As it dives, it slashes its target with its talons, knocking it to the ground.

Peregrine

Peregrine wing

Primary coverts

Long flight feathers

Secondary flight feathers

Wing tip folds back when diving.

Peregrine flight

The peregrine falcon dives for prey with its wings folded. This method of catching prey is known as "stooping."

The swift can fly continuously at an average speed of about 25 mph (40 kmph).

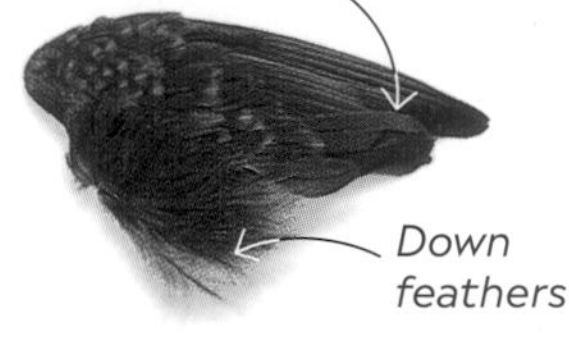

Speed in bursts

The kingfisher's fast but short flight is achieved on stubby, triangular wings.

Kingfisher flight

The kingfisher flies with whirring wing beats. It can brake in mid-air to dive for fish.

Kingfisher

Rapid transit

A migrating duck can travel up to 1,000 miles (1,600 km) in a day. Many ducks, such as the shoveler, have a colored patch on each wing called a speculum, possibly to help them identify their species when flocking.

Long-haul migrants

Many geese travel vast distances each year in order to breed. They can maintain a speed of up to 35 mph (55 kmph) for many hours without stopping. Their wings are long and broad to provide the lift needed to keep the birds airborne.

Lesser white-fronted goose

Primary coverts

Median and lesser coverts

Primary flight feathers

Shoveler wing

Speculum

Strong primary flight feathers

Beating wings

Ducks and geese beat their wings constantly during flight.

Pintail

Broad wing surface gives maximum lift for takeoff and long-distance flight.

Primary coverts

Wing point

Speculum

Waterproof wings

The pintail duck waterproofs its wings with oil produced by a gland on its back.

Lesser white-fronted goose wing

Pintail wing

Soaring, gliding, and hovering

Birds have evolved different ways of flying. Some, such as large seabirds, save energy by soaring and gliding. Other birds hover, keeping still in the air by beating their wings nonstop.

Narrow wing provides lift when gliding.

Great black-backed gull wing

Gliding gulls

Slender, pointed wings enable gulls to glide on updrafts—currents of air deflected upward by cliffs and hillsides. The lift generated by these updrafts is enough to support the great black-backed gull.

Great black-backed gull

Gull flight

In flapping flight, a gull may travel at 25 mph (40 kmph), while in a strong updraught, it can stay motionless over the ground.

Kestrel

Hanging in the air

The kestrel hovers as its sharp eyes pinpoint shrews and voles from high overhead.

Inner wing coverts mold wing to body.

Primary flight feathers reduce turbulence.

Kestrel wing

Kestrel flight

The kestrel has a fluttering forward flight typical of falcons.

Kestrel hovering

The wings beat rapidly, and the tail is fanned out to provide lift.

Up without effort

Heavy birds of prey, such as the buzzard, soar on thermals—columns of warm rising air. They only need to use flapping flight to get from one thermal to the next.

Buzzard flight

All soaring birds turn tightly to keep within the rising air of a thermal.

Buzzard wing

Broad inner feathers provide lift within a thermal.

Primary flight feathers are used for maneuvering.

Birds that cannot fly

Millions of years ago, giant flightless birds roamed Earth. Today, only a few smaller species survive.

Rhea wing

Downy feathers provide insulation but cannot produce lift.

Wings as flippers

Penguins swim by "flying" underwater with their wings. King penguins (above) can reach depths of 650 ft (200 m). Their wings act as flippers, moving them through the water.

Rhea

Powerful runners

Rheas are found in the grasslands of South America. They have fluffy plumage but no flight feathers. They can run fast to evade predators.

Penguin flipper

Stiff wing blade acts as a propeller.

Tails

Some birds, such as guillemots and puffins, have hardly any tail, while others, such as peacocks and male birds of paradise, have long, trailing tails that make flight difficult.

Rump feathers
The rump feathers above the base of a wood pigeon's tail provide insulation.

Tail coverts
Dense rows of these feathers smooth the air flow over the tail.

Tail feathers
Like most birds, the wood pigeon has 12 tail feathers.

Wood pigeon

Tips worn and frayed by flight and rubbing against the ground

AIR BRAKE

When a bird comes in to land, it lowers and fans out its tail feathers. The feathers act as a brake, slowing the bird's approach.

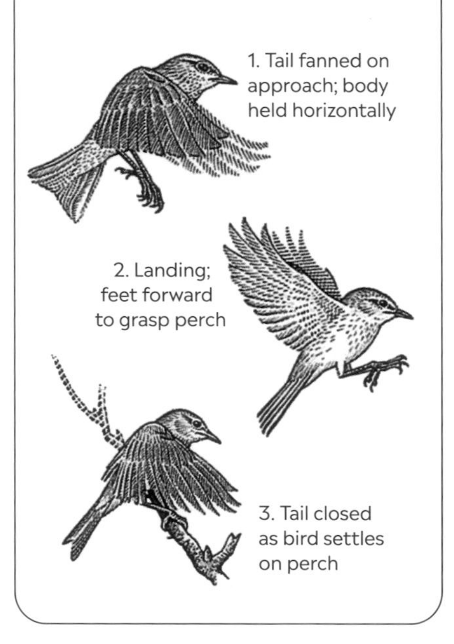

Face-off
Two male black grouse face each other in a battle to attract females. They spread their tails, call loudly, and leap in the air.

Tail shapes

Birds that spend much of their time airborne usually have light, streamlined tails. Other birds, especially those that live on the ground or in woodland, have tails that are used for balance, perching, or attracting a mate.

Forked tails
Many finches have a fork-shaped tail that helps them maneuver. Juvenile birds tend to have more sharply pointed tail tips than adult birds.

Crossbill

Rump feathers

Magpie tail

Elongated tail feathers

A tail for balance
The central feathers in a magpie's tail are nearly 10 in (25 cm) long. Long tails are usually used for display, but it is more likely that in magpies they are used for balance on the ground or when clambering in trees.

Great spotted woodpecker tail

Sharp points caused by rubbing against trees

Great spotted woodpecker

Tails for support
A woodpecker uses its stiff tail for support as it climbs a tree trunk. Its tail feathers are unusually stiff so they can support a large amount of the bird's weight.

Rump feathers

Crossbill tail

Fork-shaped tail

Some **woodpeckers** can **hit a tree trunk 20 times per second.**

Male black grouse's tail

A tail for display
The male black grouse has crescent-shaped tail feathers, while the female's tail feathers are straight. Differences like this are evidence that the shape of the tail has evolved for display rather than for fight.

The structure **of feathers**

Like hair and claws, feathers are made from a substance called keratin, which makes them strong and flexible. As feathers develop, they split apart to form a mesh of fine, parallel strands called barbs that lock together to create a smooth surface.

Breakable plumage

The central American motmot changes the shape of its tail feathers while preening. When it pecks at a feather, the barbs break off, leaving a bare shaft with a spoon-shaped tip.

HOW FEATHERS GROW

Feathers start growing as pulp inside tubes called sheaths or pins. The tip emerges from the sheath, unrolling and splitting to form a flat blade. Eventually, the sheath falls away, leaving the fully formed feather.

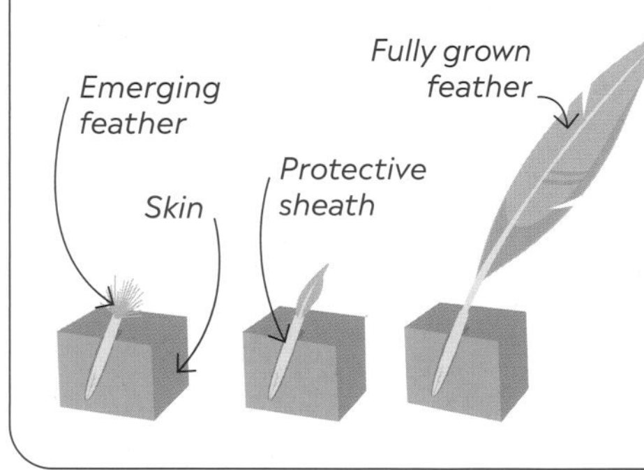

Magnification of macaw feather showing barbs and barbules

Only the parallel barbs are visible in this magnified flight feather

Feathers within feathers

Under high magnification, barbs and barbules look almost like miniature feathers.

Shaft

Downcurved edge

Barbs locked together to form a smooth surface

Hollow interior

Quill

Pulp from interior of shaft

Quill tip attached to muscles

Shaft

The hollow shaft contains the dried pulp remains.

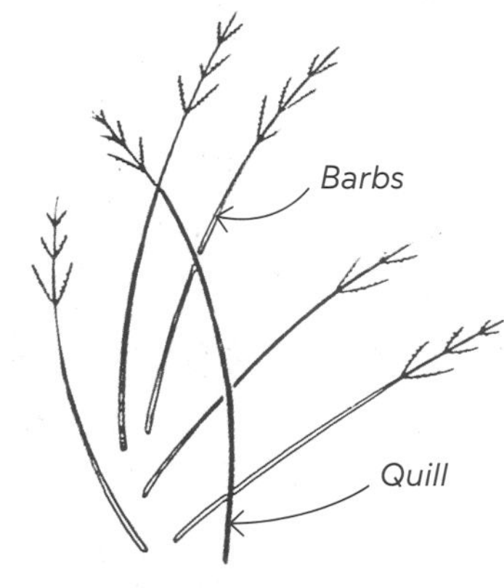

Filoplumes

These hairlike growths are found between the feathers on a bird's body.

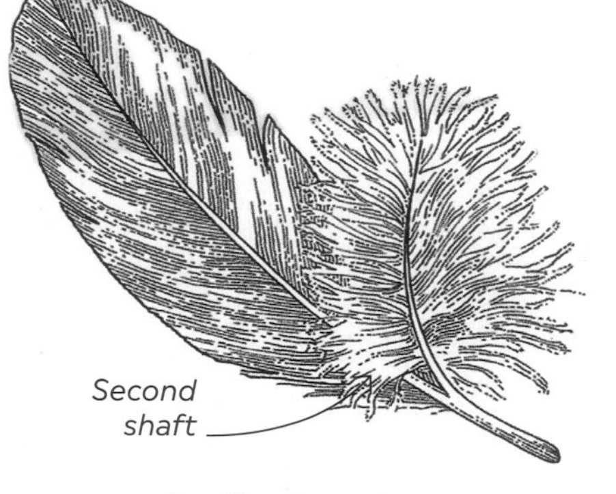

Split feathers

Some feathers split to form two different halves on the same shaft.

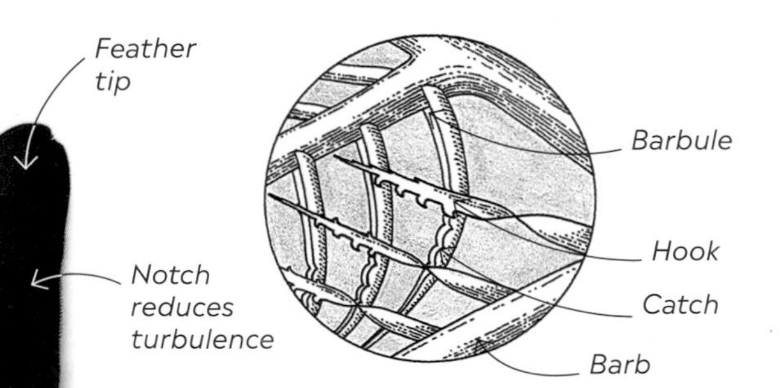

Feather-locking system

A surface for flight

To work effectively, a flight feather has to form a single continuous surface for air to flow over. This surface or vane is produced by thousands of barbules. These lie on either side of each barb and lock together as hooks and catches.

Feather care

Feathers become worn and dirty with use and are often infested with parasites. Birds spend a lot of time caring for their plumage. They do this by preening—using their beak as a comb—oiling, powdering, and bathing, both in water and in dust.

Powdered plumage
Egrets, herons, and some other birds have special feathers that disintegrate to form a powder. This powder is used to keep the plumage in good condition.

Helpful ants
Jays sometimes encourage ants to swarm over their feathers. An acid produced by the ants may dislodge parasites in the jay's plumage.

Dust baths
Bathing in dust helps clean a bird's plumage by scouring dirt from the feathers.

Feathers

The feathers that make up a bird's plumage consist of four main types—down, body, tail, and wing feathers. They come in many colored structures and shapes.

Down feathers

These soft, finely divided feathers trap a layer of air to provide warmth.

Body feathers

Also known as contour feathers, these feathers streamline a bird's body.

Tail feathers

Tail feathers, or reticles, are for steering, balance, and display.

Wing feathers

Inner wing feathers smooth the flow of air over the bird's wing. Outer wing feathers are the strongest feathers in a bird's plumage and provide power for flight. Wing feathers are collectively called remiges.

EYEWITNESS

Roxie Laybourne

US ornithologist Roxie Laybourne (1910–2003) was known as the "feather detective" because she pioneered the technique of studying feathers to solve bird-related airplane accidents. Her work has helped the aviation industry improve air safety by identifying the birds that are most likely to collide with planes.

Wing **feathers**

A bird's wing feathers (remiges) combine strength with lightness and flexibility. Compared with the rest of the body, the wings have relatively few feathers. Together, they form a perfect surface for flight.

Graded shapes
Away from the wing tip, the feathers are shorter and broader.

The outer wing

Outer wing feathers provide most of the power for flight and prevent a bird from "stalling." The outermost flight feathers can be spread open or closed up to help with steering.

Coverts
The coverts at the base of the flight feathers smooth the flow of air.

Lopsided
Most flight feathers are narrower on the leading edge to provide lift.

Heavy-duty feathers
The mute swan, which weighs up to 26 lb (12 kg), needs long, strong feathers to power its flight.

Above and below
Many wing feathers, such as these macaw feathers, have different structures on the upper surface, which makes it produce different colors.

Silent feathers
The fringed edges of owl feathers help to make flight silent.

Slotted feathers
The deep slot in this crow's feather reduces turbulence.

The inner wing

Inner wing feathers are generally shorter than those on the outer wing. They are not subject to as much force during flight, so their quills are shorter, and their feathers are less well anchored.

A balanced blade
The feathers between the inner and outer wing have curved quills and blunt tips. Inner wing feathers point away from the wind, so they do not need a lopsided shape to provide lift.

Feather from junction of wing and body

Inner flight feathers

Colored by its food
The greater flamingo eats shrimp, which have in turn eaten algae containing pigments called carotenoids. It is these pigments that give the flamingo's feathers their pink color.

Secondary feathers
Secondary feathers are broader than primary feathers and cannot be controlled as much. These help the bird lift and stay in the air.

In-flight markings
The bright colors of many birds are revealed only when their wings are fully open.

Feathers make up about **5 to 10 percent** of a **bird's weight.**

Underwing feathers
The underwing coverts lie close together to smooth the flow of air.

Infrequent fliers
The wild turkey lives on the ground and rarely uses its feathers for flight.

Sail feathers
The male mandarin duck uses its sail feathers to attract a mate.

Down, body, and **tail feathers**

Feathers are designed not only for flight. Some are used to insulate the bird's body; others are used to camouflage, to incubate the eggs, or to attract a mate. These tasks are performed by down feathers, body feathers, and the feathers in the tail.

Body feathers

Body feathers come in a variety of colors, shapes, and sizes. Some are used just to cover the bird's body, while others play a key role in courtship and display.

A pheasant's cape
The neck feathers of the male golden pheasant form a brilliant black and gold cape.

Patterns on the surface
In many birds, only the exposed tips of the feathers show distinctive markings.

Down feathers

Down feathers are found next to the bird's skin. Their barbs do not lock together but spread out to form a soft mass.

Barb

Quill

Unlocked barbs
The separate barbs in this peacock feather trap a layer of air for insulation.

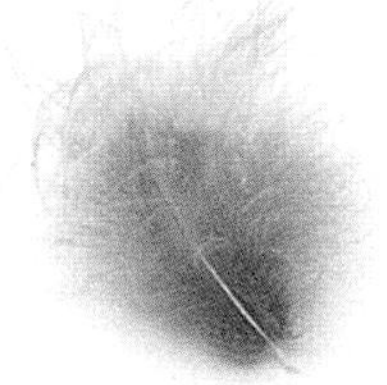

Thermal cover
Small down feathers are packed around the body to form a furlike mat.

Dual function
Many feathers also have a mass of down where they are attached to the body. These help in camouflage and also keeps the bird warm.

Incubation
Many birds, like the teal, use breast feathers to keep their eggs warm.

Tropical brilliance
Many tropical birds have brightly colored feathers that may help them identify and communicate with their own kind.

Macaw feathers

Red lory feathers

African gray parrot feathers

Leafy camouflage
The dull green tips of the green woodpecker's feathers help camouflage it in grassy fields.

Shortened barbs

Courtship plumes
These hanging feathers adorn the neck of the male wild turkey. Each feather is divided into a pair of plumes.

Flying heavyweight
This feather is from a bustard—one of the heaviest flying birds.

Tail feathers

Birds use their tail feathers to steer during flight, to balance when perched or on the ground, or to help the male attract a mate.

Eyed feathers
The "eyes" on the male peacock's tail make a splendid courtship display.

Pheasant

Long tails
The tails of male game birds like pheasants can be exceptionally long. A Japanese red jungle fowl's tail can reach up to 35 ft (10.5 m).

A curled tail
The male mallard has two distinctive curled feathers at the base of its tail. The female's tail is straight.

Bred for color
The varied colors of budgerigars are the result of controlled breeding.

Central feather
This symmetrical owl feather is from the center of the tail.

Iridescent tails
Magpies have iridescent tail feathers that look black from a distance.

Diet
The light bars—called fault bars—in this parrot's feather were due to changes in its diet as the feather was growing.

Young and old
Here, a growing kestrel's feather is shown beside a fully grown one.

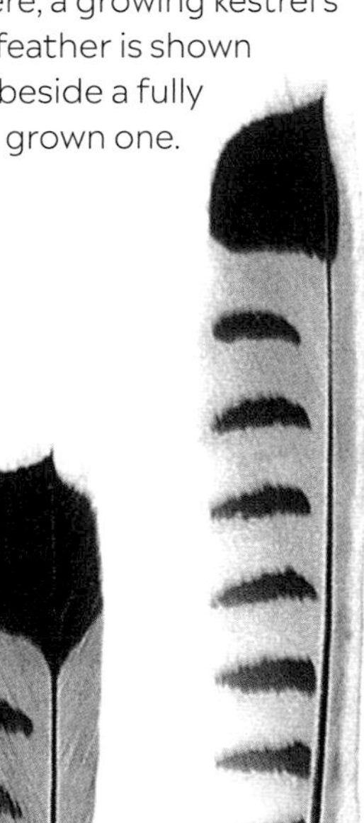

Growing feather

Mature feather

Outer tail feathers
The feathers farthest from the tail's center are less symmetrical, giving the tail a curved bar. The feathers shown below are from a curlew.

Courtship

Birds attract their mates using a variety of techniques, ranging from spectacular plumage to brightly colored legs and inflatable pouches. Some male birds use ritual movements, which vary from a gull's nod of the head to lengthy courtship ceremonies involving bizarre dancing displays.

Role reversal

Unusually for a bird, the female red-necked phalarope courts the male, and the male looks after the eggs.

The peacock's tail

Peacocks display some of the most spectacular courtship plumage in the bird world.

Hidden support

From the back, the upright feathers of the male peacock's "true" tail can be seen. These support the much longer and more brilliant tail coverts.

On parade

Male lyrebirds make themselves arenas on which they strut and display.

Eye-catching feathers

To attract a mate, the male Raggiana bird of paradise performs a beautiful bowing dance and throws his plumes wide open.

Inflatable pouch

The male frigate bird keeps his brilliant red throat pouch inflated for many hours to attract a mate.

Long, hooked beak aids in catching fish

Dancing on water

Great crested grebes perform a sequence of bizarre courtship dances. They begin with a head-shaking dance before diving to collect beakfuls of water weed. The birds then paddle furiously as they present the weed to each other.

Defusing tension

Although boobies nest in densely packed colonies, each bird will stab at any neighbor that dares to intrude on its private territory. When pairs meet, they jab and touch each other's bill to defuse aggressive instincts.

Bright beak

The brilliant colors on puffins' beaks are at their brightest during the breeding season. The color lies in a horny sheath covering the outside of the beak that drops off in the fall.

Miniature rivals

Although tiny, male hummingbirds fiercely defend their territories.

Ringed plover

Camouflage

When confronted by danger, most birds immediately take to the air. But some, particularly those that feed or roost on the ground, use camouflage to hide from predators. The birds that lie low the longest are those with camouflaged plumage.

Hidden on pebbles

An open beach may seem to be a difficult place for a bird to conceal itself. But the moment it stops moving, a ringed plover appears to vanish among the beach pebbles.

Woodcock

First defense

The woodcock is mainly nocturnal and lives in woodland. It covers the white underside of its tail feathers to stay hidden. If its camouflage fails, it will take off and dart through the trees with a swerving flight.

Probing beak

Seasonal changes

In winter, some birds, such as the ptarmigan, change color to blend in with the snowy landscape. As birds molt their feathers every year, the ptarmigan can change color by shedding one set of feathers and replacing them with another different-colored set.

In summer, the ptarmigan's brown feathers hide it against the rocks.

In winter, its white plumage blends in with the snow.

Nightjar

Debris on woodland floor

Wood-coloured feathers help it to merge with its surroundings.

Daytime hideout

The nightjar feeds on insects at dusk, but during the day, it sits completely still, looking like a broken branch. It keeps the white patch on its wing hidden in order to stay camouflaged.

Feet and **tracks**

Birds' feet are greatly variable in size and shape, depending on where the birds live and how they find food. Most have only three or four toes, while the ostrich has just two. Birds that rarely land, such as swifts, have small legs, making it hard for them to walk, but they are able to climb into cavities for nesting.

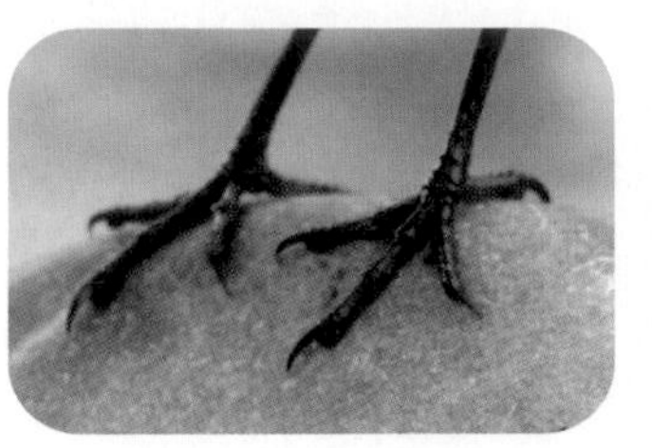

Wagtail feet

Thrush feet

For perching

Perching birds have a single hind toe. This toe enables the birds to tightly grasp the branches on which they perch.

All-purpose feet

Crows are perching birds. Their feet have hooked claws and a large hind toe.

Crow foot

Hind toe

Hooked claws

Greater spotted woodpecker foot

Rear toes

Green woodpecker foot

Front toes

Claws for climbing

Woodpeckers' feet, used for gripping trees, have two toes pointing forward and two pointing backward.

Outspread owl foot

Narrow crow foot

Different uses

Birds of prey spread their toes to catch prey, while the crow keeps its toes closer together.

Birds of prey

These birds have long talons and are so highly adapted to grasping prey that they have difficulty walking.

Sparrowhawk

Talons

Grip

The eagle's grip allows it to carry heavy prey below its body.

Saw-whet owl foot

Saw-whet owl

Insulating feathers

Talons

Feathered talons

The feathers that cover the legs and feet of most owls help silence their approach as they swoop down on prey.

Waders

Wading birds have long toes to prevent them from sinking into soft mud.

Moorhen foot

Elongated, widely spread toes

Lily-trotter

Jacanas can walk over floating plants on their long, thin toes.

Flanged feet

The coot has double flanges of scaly skin that extend from the toe bones. During swimming, the flanges open out as the foot moves backward, and closes as it moves forward.

Coot foot

Scaly flange aids swimming

Coot

Canada goose foot

Webbed toes for swimming

Webbed feet

Ducks, geese, swans, gulls, and many seabirds have webbed feet for efficient swimming. Petrels can almost "walk" on water by pattering with their webbed feet and flapping their wings, while waterfowl use their feet as waterbrakes when landing.

Nuthatch landing

Legs for perching

Perching birds have a special mechanism to prevent them from falling off perches. When a perching bird lands on a branch, its weight makes its leg tendons tighten and clamp its toes tightly shut. To take off, the bird contracts its toe muscles, the foot springs open, and it can then fly away.

Perching bird's leg

Thigh bone

Ankle joint

Toes clamp to perch when the bird rests its weight on the foot.

Bird tracks

Birds move on the ground in one of two ways. Many smaller birds hop, as they can easily lift their body weight by flexing their feet. Larger birds cannot hop and so walk instead.

Tracks in mud
Bird tracks are best seen in wet mud and fresh snow.

Walking tracks
Instead of hopping, large birds transfer their weight from foot to foot by walking.

Goose tracks

Finch tracks

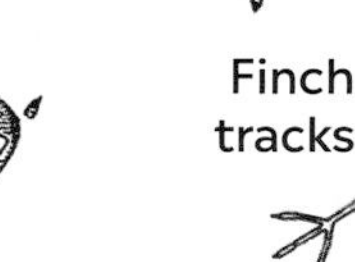

Hopping tracks
Small birds, particularly those that live in woodland, hop on the ground.

The **senses**

Birds live in a world that is dominated by sight and sound. From high overhead, a hovering kestrel can see the ground below in intricate detail. Birds also have excellent hearing—they can distinguish notes that are far too fast for humans to separate. Some birds, such as vultures and albatrosses, use their sense of smell to track their food.

The raven is a member of the crow family

Long flight wings

Raven skull

Cranium

Nostril cavity

Bone at base of eye socket supports eye

Eye socket points sideways

Ear opening, usually hidden by feathers

Senses and the skull

In birds, the bony plates of the cranium are fused together to form a strong, lightweight case. The eyes are often bigger than the brain and are held in their sockets by tiny bones attached to the eyeball.

Intelligence

Like humans, some birds can solve tasks with the help of tools and maintain complex social lives. Parrots are known to mimic many sounds, including human speech, while some species of heron use bait, such as an insect, to catch fish. Some crows can even use twigs as tools to hook insects out of cavities.

Opposed eyes for wide-angle vision

Snipe skull

Bird vision

Most hunting birds can assess distances with great accuracy. Owls' eyes point almost directly forward, giving a wide field of binocular vision. Although they cannot swivel their eyeballs, they can turn their necks to point backward. Birds that are themselves hunted tend to have eyes that point in opposite directions. Most waders, for example, have sideways-facing eyes, which allow them a view of 360 degrees.

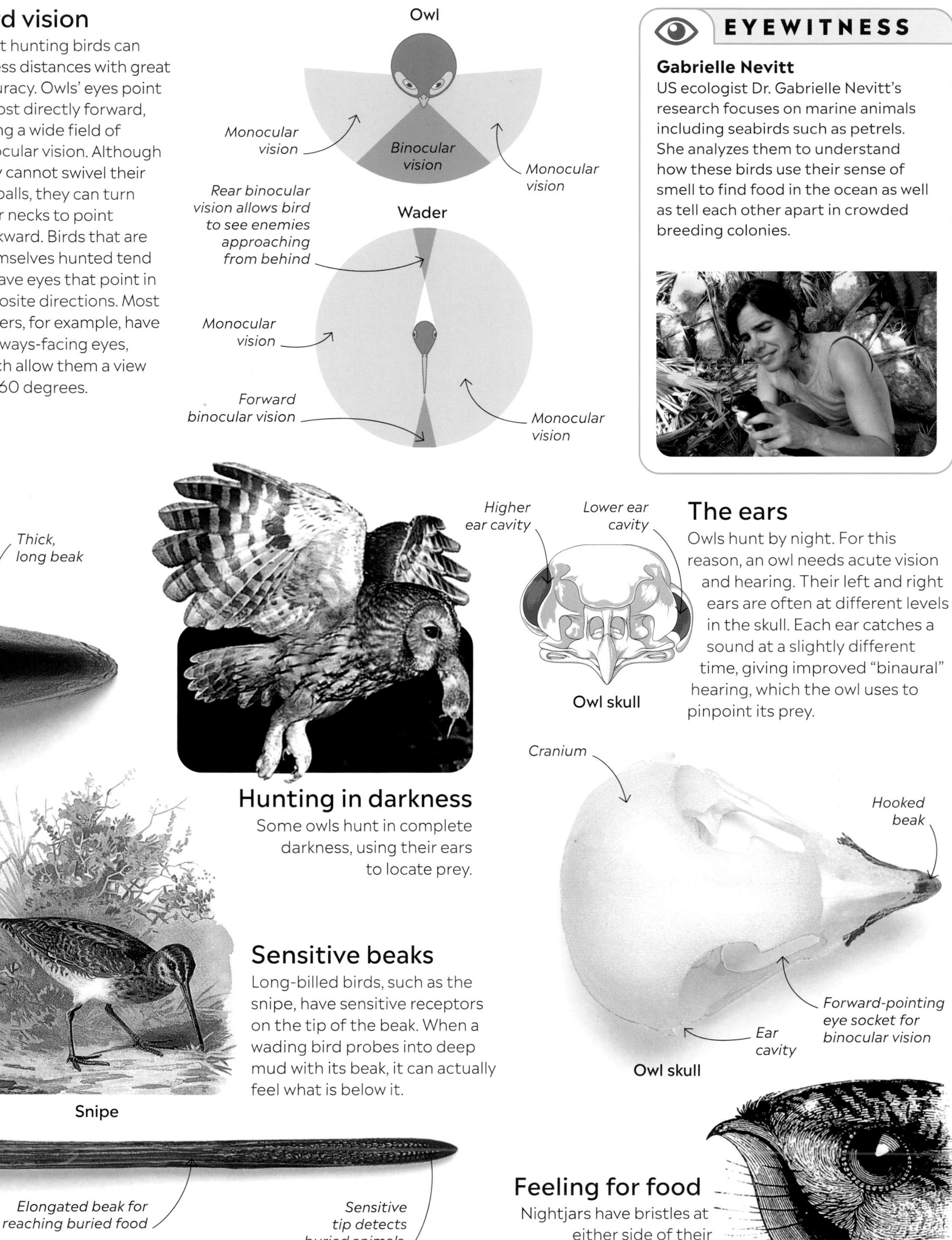

EYEWITNESS

Gabrielle Nevitt

US ecologist Dr. Gabrielle Nevitt's research focuses on marine animals including seabirds such as petrels. She analyzes them to understand how these birds use their sense of smell to find food in the ocean as well as tell each other apart in crowded breeding colonies.

The ears

Owls hunt by night. For this reason, an owl needs acute vision and hearing. Their left and right ears are often at different levels in the skull. Each ear catches a sound at a slightly different time, giving improved "binaural" hearing, which the owl uses to pinpoint its prey.

Hunting in darkness

Some owls hunt in complete darkness, using their ears to locate prey.

Sensitive beaks

Long-billed birds, such as the snipe, have sensitive receptors on the tip of the beak. When a wading bird probes into deep mud with its beak, it can actually feel what is below it.

Feeling for food

Nightjars have bristles at either side of their mouths, which may help them feel for food.

Beaks

Their front limbs are completely adapted for flight, so most birds hold their food with their beaks alone. Birds' beaks have evolved into a variety of shapes to tackle different kinds of food. Some are short and straight for probing, while others are long and curved for picking out food.

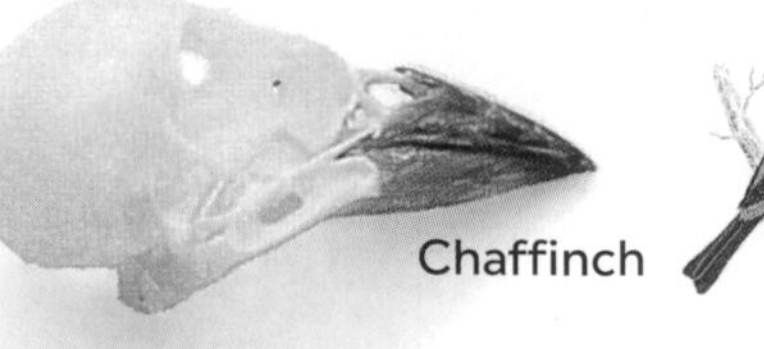

Seed-cracker

Birds such as chaffinches, which live on hard seeds, have short cone-shaped beaks to crack open their food.

A woodpecker's beak is strong enough for hammering, and its tip can repair itself.

The curlew's forceps

The curlew jabs its long beak into soft mud to pull out worms and mollusks that are beyond the reach of other birds.

Curled, long beak

Curlew

A tweezer beak

The blackbird's long, pointed beak enables it to pick up small seeds and grasp larger food items, such as earthworms.

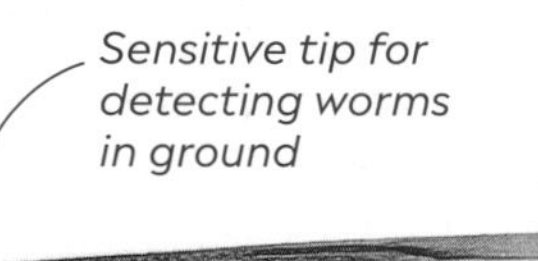

Sensitive tip for detecting worms in ground

Long beak

Woodcock

For marshes and woodland

The woodcock uses its long, pointed beak to extract earthworms and insect larvae from damp ground.

Blackbird

Pointed beak for grasping seeds and larger food

Kestrel

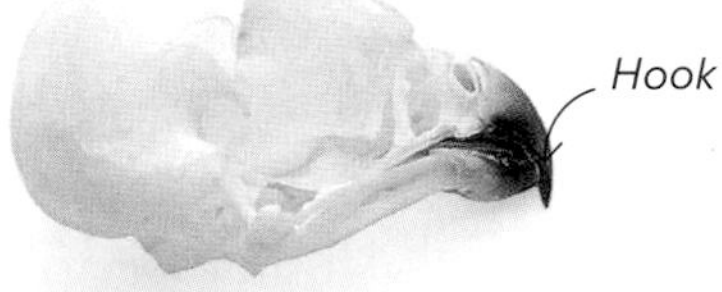

Meat-eater's beak

The kestrel's hooked beak enables it to pull apart animals that are too big to be swallowed whole.

Merganser

"Teeth" made from horny material

Sawlike duck bills

Unlike mammals, birds do not have teeth. However, some birds, such as the merganser, have sawlike structures on the sides of their beaks that are used for catching fish.

Parrot *Hook*

Fruit-eater's beak

The parrot uses the hook at the tip of its beak to extract fruit pulp, while its jaws are used to crack open seeds. Parrots also use their feet to hold and turn their food while they crack it open.

Nostril

Long, hooked beak

All-purpose beak

Gulls' long beaks end in a hook. This enables them to pull apart their food and hold prey, like fish along the length of their beaks.

Gull

Hinge of lower bill and skull

The upper bill has a ridge to trap food.

Lower bill

Underwater sieve

The flamingo uses its large beak to sieve animals and plants from the water. The lower bill moves up and down to pump water against the top bill, where a row of fine slits traps the food.

Plant- and invertebrate-eaters

The majority of birds live on food that is incredibly abundant. This includes seeds, grass, nectar, insects, worms, and many other small animals.

Eating plants and seeds

They have no teeth, so birds have to crush plants and seeds before they digest them. They do this with their powerful beaks and a muscular organ called the gizzard, which grinds the food into pulp.

Hard-cased seeds

Finch skull

Seed-eaters
Finches have short, sharp bills to break open seeds and nuts, although almost all of them feed invertebrates to their chicks.

Goose skull

Leaves

Grain

Pigeon skull

Feeding on crops
Pigeons and doves feed on seeds and leaves. Unlike all other birds, pigeons' pointed bills enable them to drink without tilting their head back.

Broad bill for tearing grass

Living on grass
Geese live on a diet of grass. Because it passes through their digestive system in just two hours, they need to feed almost constantly.

Capercaillie skull

Hooked beak for grasping leaves

Conifer-eaters
Species such as pheasants, grouse, and capercaillie from Northern Europe eat whatever plant food is available, although their preference is for seeds. In winter, the capercaillie feeds on the leaves of conifer trees.

Seeds

Needles of conifer trees

Grass and waterplants eaten by geese

Invertebrate-eaters

Many birds alter their diet throughout the year and eat whatever food is available. The number of insects and other invertebrates—animals without backbones—increases dramatically in spring, whereas in winter, food is scarcer and consists mainly of larvae (grubs) in wood or in the soil.

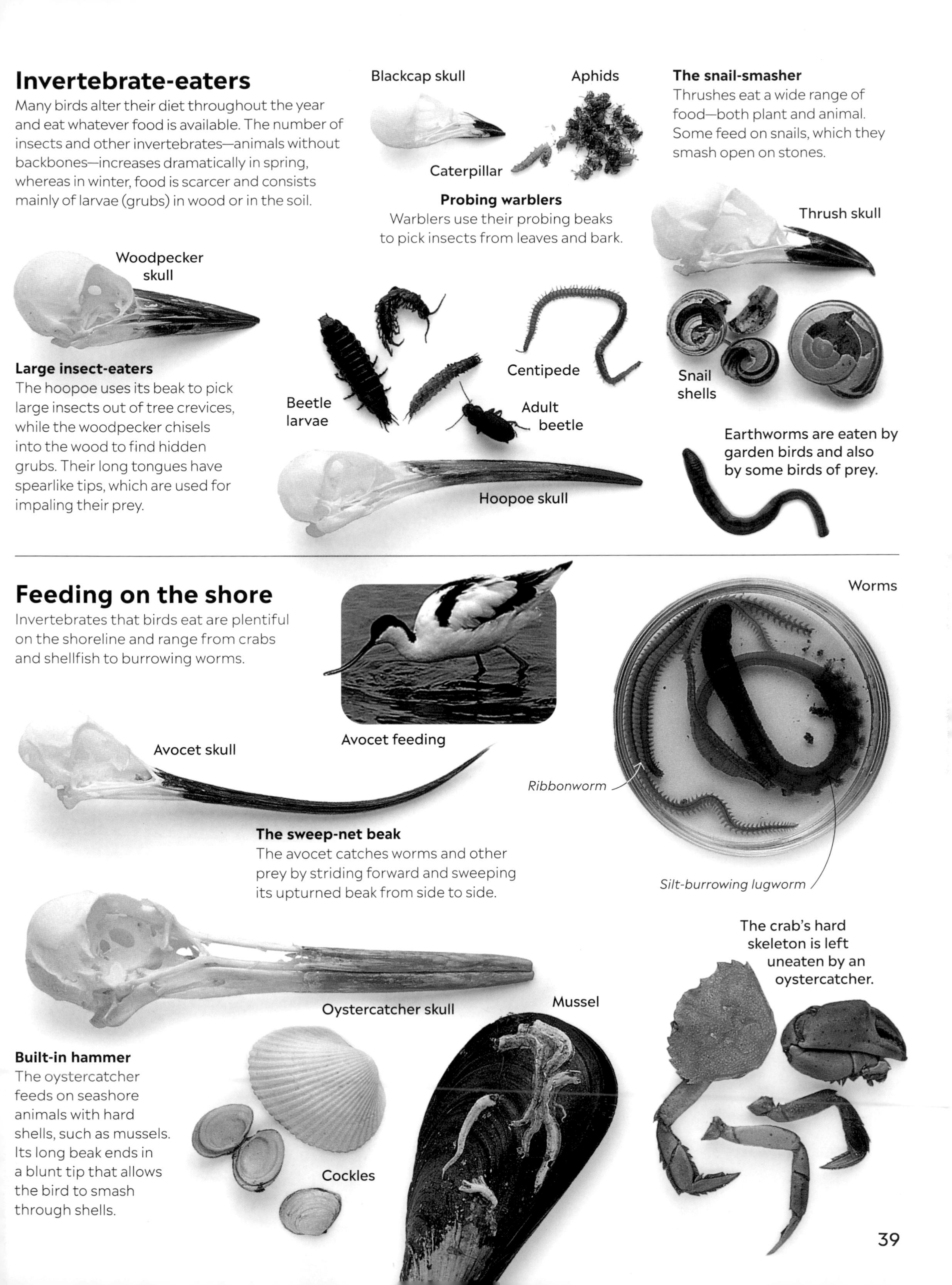

Probing warblers
Warblers use their probing beaks to pick insects from leaves and bark.

The snail-smasher
Thrushes eat a wide range of food—both plant and animal. Some feed on snails, which they smash open on stones.

Large insect-eaters
The hoopoe uses its beak to pick large insects out of tree crevices, while the woodpecker chisels into the wood to find hidden grubs. Their long tongues have spearlike tips, which are used for impaling their prey.

Earthworms are eaten by garden birds and also by some birds of prey.

Feeding on the shore

Invertebrates that birds eat are plentiful on the shoreline and range from crabs and shellfish to burrowing worms.

The sweep-net beak
The avocet catches worms and other prey by striding forward and sweeping its upturned beak from side to side.

The crab's hard skeleton is left uneaten by an oystercatcher.

Built-in hammer
The oystercatcher feeds on seashore animals with hard shells, such as mussels. Its long beak ends in a blunt tip that allows the bird to smash through shells.

Hunters and **fishers**

Flight enables birds to cover great distances in search of food. Few animals, either on land or far out at sea, are beyond their reach. A dead animal or a field of crops is quickly spotted by passing birds and turned into a satisfying meal.

Strips of meat torn from prey

Tawny owl skull

Fur is later discarded in pellets

Buzzard skull

Night and day hunters

Birds of prey, such as the buzzard, catch rodents and larger mammals during the day, while owls mostly hunt during the night.

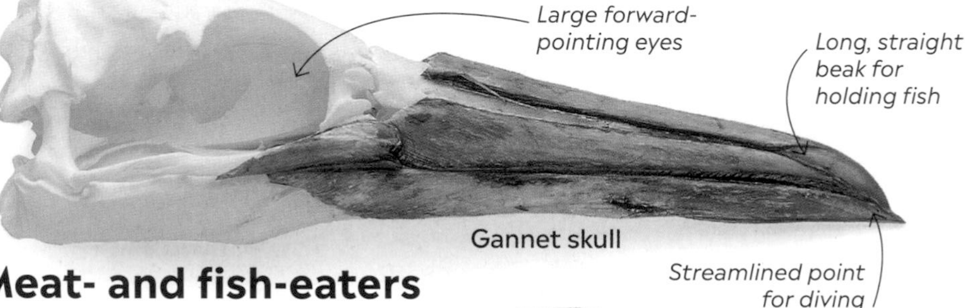

Gannet skull

Meat- and fish-eaters

Most fish-eaters use their beaks to catch prey. On land, meat-eaters use their talons for catching small mammals and their beaks for tearing flesh.

Cormorant skull

Stealth

The heron stays still until its prey swims within reach of its stabbing beak.

Above and below water

Gannets have binocular vision, which helps them track food sources before they plummet underwater. They dive-bomb shoals of fish by plunging, with their wings folded, from heights of up to 100 ft (30 m). They stay below the surface for only a few seconds.

A mixed diet

Birds that survive on a mixed diet take advantage of any meal that comes their way. These scavengers thrive on waste food and household trash as well as more natural food items.

Ever-adaptable crows

Crows are among the most successful generalist feeders in the bird world. They have a bold, inquisitive nature, together with a strong, all-purpose beak. Insects, dead birds, live mammals, worms, and seeds are all part of their diet.

Magpie skull

Crow skull

Jay skull

EYEWITNESS

Alexander Bond

Canadian biologist Alexander Bond focuses on how plastics in the marine environment are eaten by seabirds, and the devastating effect this has on their populations. Alexander also champions LGBTQIA+ inclusion in conservation biology.

A freshwater opportunist

The small, aggressive coot lives by lakes and rivers. It eats any water life it can find, including weeds, snails, tadpoles, fish, and even young ducklings.

Coot skull

Invertebrates and insects

Earthworm

Egg broken open after being stolen from nest

Seeds

Nuts eaten by birds have rough-edged holes.

Water snails from slow-moving fresh water

Animals and plants eaten by coots in shallow ponds

Gannets can fly over water at an average speed of 10 mph (15 kmph).

Pellets

They have no teeth, so predatory birds like owls cannot chew their food. Instead, they rip their prey apart or eat it whole. This means that they swallow large amounts of indigestible bones, fur, and feathers. They regurgitate these items in the form of pellets.

Pellets in open ground

The pellets of the short-eared owl are cylindrical, with rounded ends. This owl does not drop its pellets from a perch but scatters them on tufts of grass.

Rounded ends

Rodent limb bone

Blunt ends

Smooth dark crust

Beneath a roost

The smooth pellets of the barn owl are often found in small piles beneath roosts in barns.

Recent pellet

Older pellet starting to disintegrate

Protruding bone

Pointed ends

Bones and fur

Tawny owls eat shrews, mice, voles, and smaller birds. Their smooth pellets often have pointed ends. Older pellets often crumble to reveal a mass of protruding bones and tangled fur.

Earth and fur

Beetle wing-case

Beetle leg

A varied diet

These pellets are from little owls. The smaller pellets contain earth, produced by a meal of earthworms, and fur. The larger pellets reveal beetle legs and wing-cases among the earth and fur.

Shell fragments

Seed-cases mixed with shell fragments

Wader pellets

Wading bird pellets often contain shell fragments.

Crow pellets

Crow pellets often contain insect remains and plant stalks.

Songbird pellets

This songbird pellet contains metal foil among the seeds.

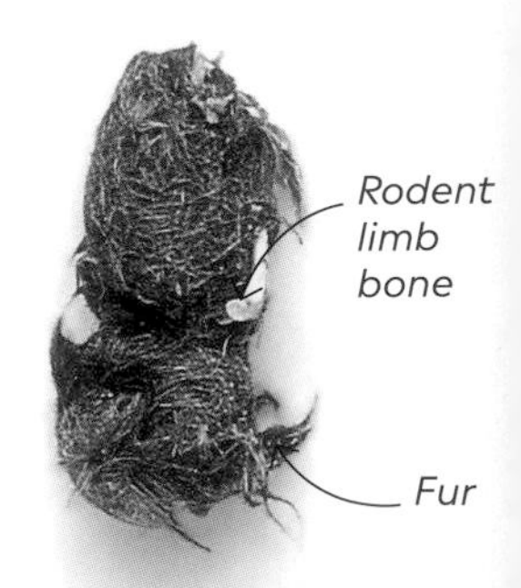

Falcon pellets

Falcon pellets contain bird, mammal, and insect remains.

Inside an owl pellet

Here, two tawny owl pellets have been taken apart. The first pellet shows that the owl had dined entirely on voles—three of these small mammals made up the bird's nightly catch. The second pellet (below) reveals starling bones, showing that birds are also a part of the tawny owl's diet.

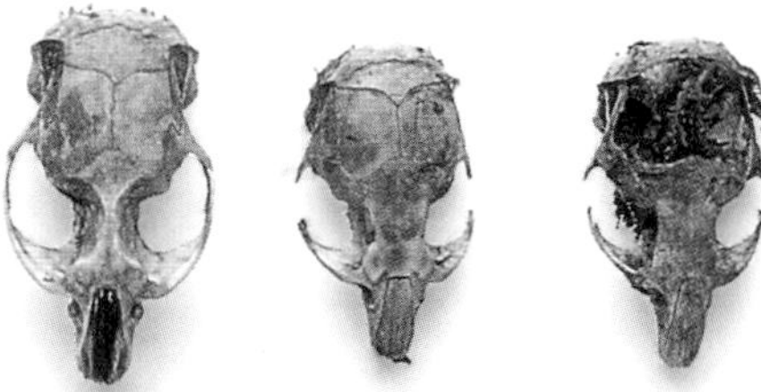

Three vole skulls, two still intact

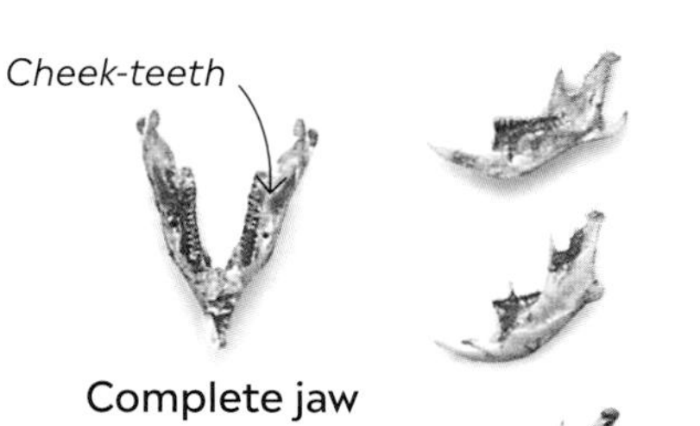

Complete jaw

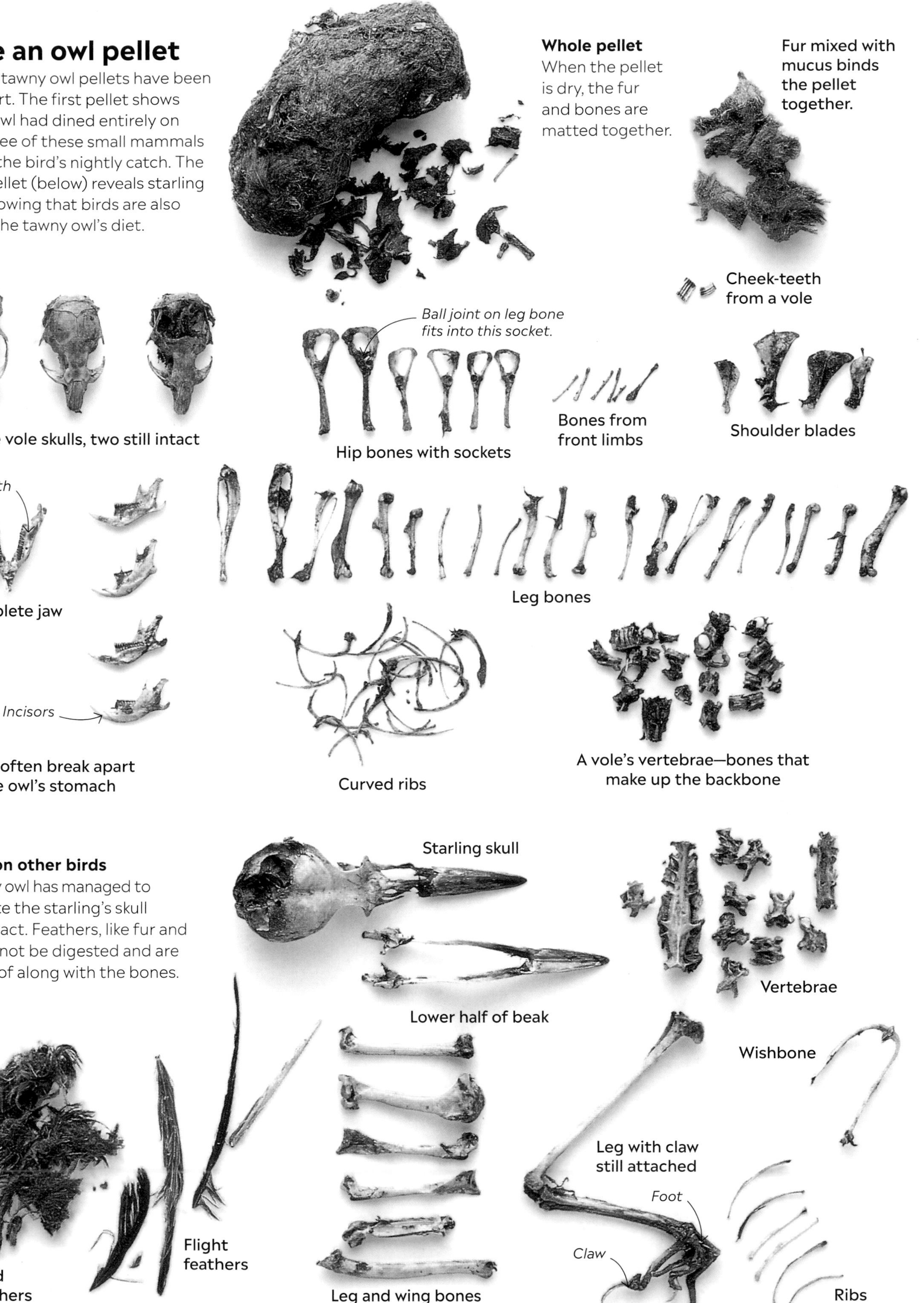

Feeding on other birds

This tawny owl has managed to regurgitate the starling's skull almost intact. Feathers, like fur and claws, cannot be digested and are disposed of along with the bones.

Making **a nest**

Many birds lay their eggs in a warm cup of material called a nest. To make a cup-shaped nest, the bird pushes the materials it has gathered loosely into place. It then sits in the center of the nest and begins to turn around and around, pushing downward and outward with its breast. This circular movement, which gives the inside of the nest its shape, is shared by all birds.

Fur and hair for insulation

Dry grass seed heads to form structure

Natural materials

Most hedgerow and woodland birds use sticks to build their nests and line them with feathers, seed heads, or animal fur. House martins and some swallows make their nests entirely from mud.

Twigs and sticks Main structural material in larger nests

Mud Mixed with saliva to form a paste

Leaves and needles Used for the inside of many cup nests

Seed heads Used in the nest lining for insulation

Human-made materials

Anything that can be carried away may end up in a bird's nest—even metal and plastic.

String Small lengths are used in many nests.

Metal foil Often collected by crows and magpies

Plastic twine A favorite with birds nesting on farmland

Paper Found in the nests of many city birds

Nest ingredients

The pied wagtail scours fields, hedgerows, and fences for plant and animal materials. It makes hundreds or perhaps thousands of trips to bring all that it has collected back to the growing nest.

Cozy nest
Packed with a huge variety of ingredients, the pied wagtail's nest displays the materials found in the bird's habitat.

Feathers for insulation

Moss for insulation

Feathers
These are collected from the ground, sometimes around fox kills, and from old nests.

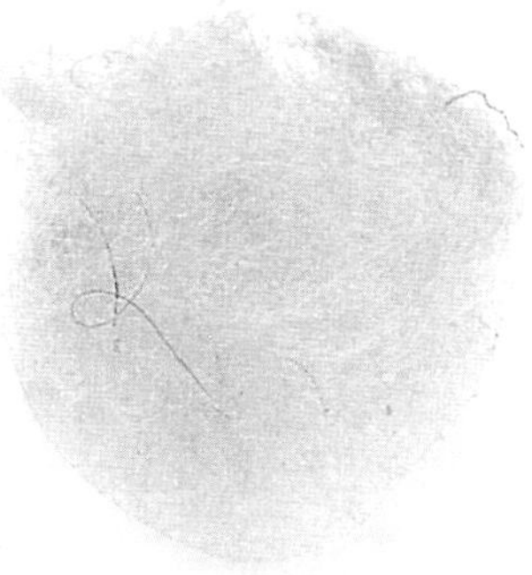

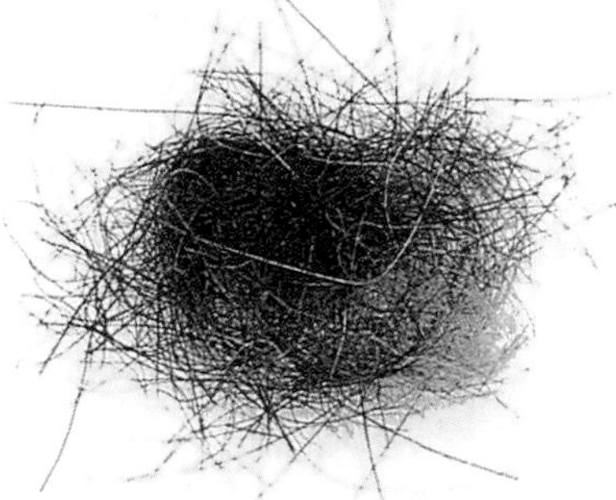

Cattle hair
Insulating hair is collected from fences and bushes.

Wool
Tufts of wool are removed from barbed wire.

Moss
Moss traps air and prevents heat loss —essential for the protection of young nestlings.

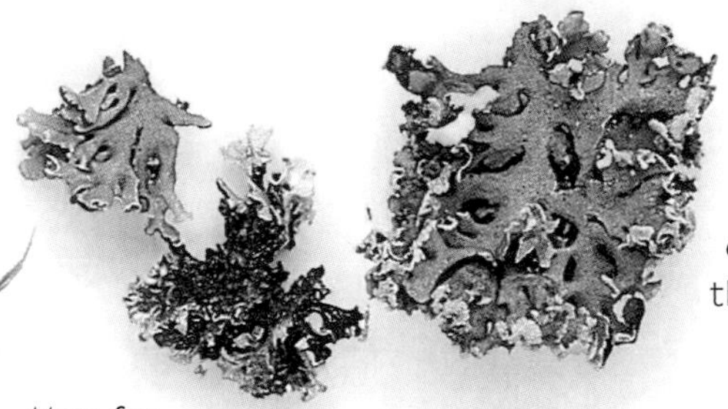

Lichen
Lichen from walls and branches helps camouflage the nest.

Grass
Seed heads and leaves help structure the nest.

Horse hair
Coarse hair from a horse's tail helps form the cup shape.

Cup **nests**

Bird nests range from tiny shelves of saliva that are glued to cave walls to massive piles of branches that can weigh as much as a car. But the most familiar nests are the cup-shaped nests, built by birds of woodland, hedgerows, and farmland.

Chaffinch with its young

Moss and lichen cup forms the nest structure.

Hair and feather lining insulates the eggs and nestlings.

Chaffinch nest

A chaffinch builds its nest by looping strands of spiders' webs around a group of forked branches. Once these anchors are secure, it builds up a cup shape with moss, lichen, and grass. It then lines the inside with feathers and hair.

Feathers from other birds provide insulation.

Dried moss

Redstart

Feather lining

Feathers are used to provide insulation. Songbirds, such as the redstart, collect feathers shed by other birds, while waders and waterfowl use their own feathers.

Mud lining

Outer cup

Song thrush feeding young

Mud lining

Many cup-nest builders use mud to line their nests. The song thrush makes a strong outer cup of twigs and grass, then lines the inside with a layer of mud mixed with saliva and animal droppings. Once applied, the lining becomes hard and can withstand rain for many months.

Nests on buildings

Some birds, particularly house martins, swifts, swallows, and storks, build their nests in stone and brick houses. Walls and window ledges make an ideal home for cliff-nesting birds, while rooftops and chimneys are used by birds that originally nested in treetops.

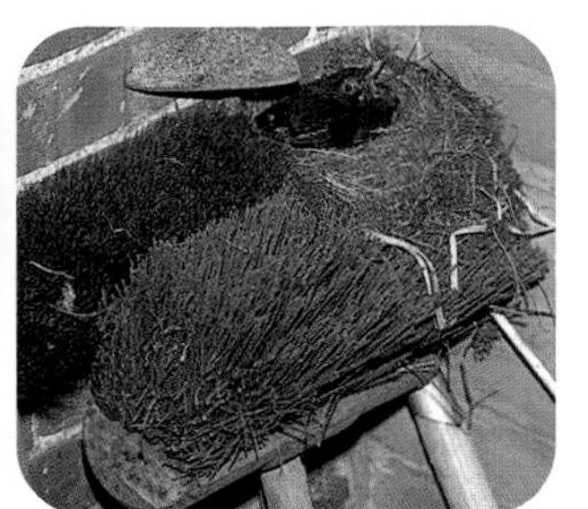

Hedgerow birds pick sites by height—this blackbird has chosen a broom.

Tree substitute
Some storks pile up their stick nests on chimneys and the tops of buildings.

EYEWITNESS

Purnima Devi Barman
Indian biologist Purnima Devi Barman has helped conserve greater adjutant storks in Assam, India. She formed a group of more than 10,000 women living in rural areas who saved nesting colonies by teaching other villagers about the birds. This discouraged people from cutting down trees where the storks nested.

Nightingale in the nest

Ready for recycling
This nightingale's loosely made nest is formed of leaves, grass, and reeds. Loose nests may be dismantled by other birds for "recycling" after their owners have left.

Loosely made cup-shaped nest

Grass lining on inside of cup

Lining made of hair collected from ferns and bark against which animals have rubbed

Outer cup made of grass, leaves, and stems

A hair-filled nest
Reed buntings build small cup-shaped nests on or near the ground. The female first builds a frame of thick grass. She then adds a lining of fur or hair, plucked from hedgerows or barbed wire.

Female reed bunting at nest

Unusual **nests**

Birds' nests vary hugely in size and structure. Some birds nest in simple hollows (scraps) in the ground, while others weave nests of astounding complexity. Nest building is entirely instinctive; although a bird gets better with practice, it needs no training.

Baltimore oriole perching above its distinctive baglike nest

String nest

This baglike nest, built by the Baltimore oriole, is made of cattle hair and string. The bird has skillfully wound some string around a twig to form a support.

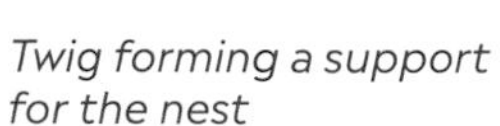

String

Cattle hair

Weaver at work

Weaver nests begin as a knotted ring, which is then extended downward to form a spherical chamber. An entrance funnel may then be added.

Shared housing

Colonial nests, although never quite this elegant, are built by a variety of birds.

Home security

This incredible nest is built by a West African weaver bird. Its long trumpet shape prevents predatory snakes from crawling inside.

Nest chamber

Entrance funnel to deter snakes

Grasses woven together to form a tube

Social weavers

This elaborate bell-shaped nest is made by the male village weaver. When finished, he flutters around the nest to entice a mate to move in. Like most weavers, the village weaver is highly social—hundreds of birds often build their nests in the same tree.

Thorn tree twig

Nest chamber

Entrance

Grass strands

Nest made of reed flowers, grasses, and feathers

Basket nest

The reed warbler's nest hangs between dried stems deep in a reed bed. The nest is anchored with "handles" similar to those on a basket.

Reeds

Feathers

Entrance hole

Interlocking mixture of moss, hair, and spider webs

Nest of long-tailed tit

Tight fit

The long-tailed tit's nest is made up of moss, hair, and spider webs and is lined with tiny feathers. However, it is so cramped that the male or female can only fit inside by curling their tail against the nest.

Eggs of waterbirds **and waders**

Seabirds that only come ashore to breed usually lay a single egg on a rocky ledge. Wading birds lay camouflaged eggs, to protect them on exposed coasts and estuaries.

A tern's eggs

Little terns usually lay their eggs in rocks. The eggs' delicate pattern hides them among the pebbles.

Fostered eggs

A moorhen may dump its eggs into the nests of other moorhens. After this, it settles down to raise up to a dozen of its own eggs itself.

Important information

It is illegal to collect or handle wild birds' eggs.

Undersized egg

Normal egg

Variations in size

A clutch of eggs sometimes contains an undersized specimen. These two eggs are both from a shoveler duck.

Eggs under guard

Common terns fiercely protect their eggs by diving directly at intruders.

Gull eggs

The great black-backed gull lays its eggs on the ground. Their speckled pattern hides them from predators.

Pointed shape

The guillemot produces one of the most strikingly shaped and variably colored eggs of all birds. Guillemots do not build nests. Instead, each female lays its single egg directly on a bare cliff ledge.

Cream and brown form

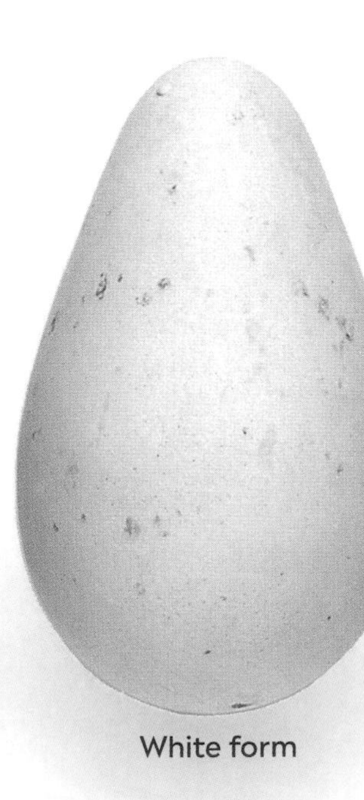

White form

Streaked gray form

Guillemot

Distraction

The little ringed plover lays its eggs on gravel or rocks for camouflage. If an intruder approaches the nest, the parents rely on the camouflage to protect the eggs from predators.

Slow developer

The fulmar's single egg needs to incubate for seven and a half weeks before it hatches.

Egg from dark clutch

Egg from light clutch

Egg from speckled clutch

Woodcock

Colors in a clutch

Each of these three eggs comes from a woodcock. The pattern and color of camouflaged eggs can vary widely between clutches.

Double points

The great crested grebe lays its long and narrow eggs on a mound of water-logged vegetation.

Curlew

Curlew egg

Curlews lay their eggs on the ground. One end of the egg is pointed, and the other is blunt.

In the treetops

The gray heron builds its nest high in the trees. When fresh, this egg was bright blue.

By water

Divers are fish-eating waterbirds. They lay their dark brown eggs by the water's edge.

Record incubation

The albatross lays the largest and heaviest egg of any seabird. Its eggs also have the longest incubation period. The parents sit on a single egg for two and a half months.

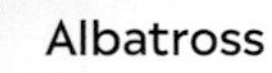

Albatross

Eggs of **land birds**

Small land birds, such as the seed- and insect-eaters, lay small eggs, often in large clutches. Large birds often lay far fewer eggs. For birds such as eagles, one small clutch a year is all they produce.

Well hidden

The nightingale's brown eggs are well concealed in tangled bushes.

Coal tit egg

Blue tit egg

Heavy clutch

Tits lay up to 15 eggs. Each clutch weighs up to a third more than the bird itself.

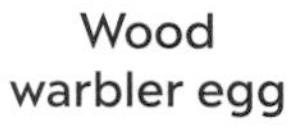

Wood warbler egg

Marsh warbler egg

Summer visitors

Most warblers migrate to breed. They time their arrival to coincide with the annual insect population explosion, which provides food for the average family of six nestlings.

Chaffinch egg

Hawfinch egg

Slow beginners

Some finches do not lay their eggs until early summer, when more seeds are available.

Tawny owl egg

Some of the museum specimens here have lost their original color.

Little owl egg

Highly visible

Owl eggs are white with a glossy surface. Their round shape is typical of many eggs laid in holes.

Baltimore oriole

Streaks

The streaks on the Baltimore oriole's egg are formed only a few hours before it is laid. The egg's pattern blends with the nest.

Less to lay

Wood pigeons lay two eggs that together weigh less than a tenth of the parent.

Chimney nest

The jackdaw lays its eggs in holes—in trees, rocky outcrops, or even chimneys.

Normal egg

Outsize egg

Carrion crow

Abnormal eggs

During the process of egg production, things sometimes go wrong. A single egg may have two yolks, or it may be of a different size than a normal egg. The eggs shown here are crow's eggs.

Brown or reddish spots

Moorland camouflage

Blotches of color help hide this grouse egg among the heather.

Cuckoo egg

Robin egg

Cuckoo

Cuckoos lay their small eggs in the nests of other birds. A cuckoo has tried to match the color of its egg with those of a robin.

A poor match

The European cuckoo has too many hosts to match all their eggs.

American robin

This bird is a member of the thrush family, unlike the European robin.

Nonstop production

If conditions are good, a female blackbird can lay up to five clutches of four eggs in a season, although few offspring survive the winter.

A female cuckoo can lay up to 23 eggs in other birds' nests.

On the ground

The nocturnal nightjar lays its pair of eggs on rough ground.

Hole-nester

Many woodpeckers chisel out holes in trees for their glossy eggs.

In the city

The kestrel sometimes nests on city buildings, where its eggs perch on rooftops.

Vulnerable hawks

Sparrowhawks, like most birds of prey, lay eggs that can be camouflaged easily. The eggs are bright blue when laid, but the color fades.

Varied colors

The fish-eating osprey produces eggs of varied colors.

On rocky cliffs

The Egyptian vulture lays its eggs high upon cliffs and in cave mouths.

One of a pair

Eagles wait several days between laying their first and second eggs.

Slow developers

Buzzard eggs take more than five weeks to be incubated. The young stay in the nest for another six weeks.

Extraordinary **eggs**

The largest living bird, the ostrich, lays an egg that is 4,500 times heavier than that of the smallest, the hummingbird. In the past, one of the heaviest birds that ever existed—the elephant bird—laid eggs that could each have contained seven ostrich eggs with room to spare.

The roc

This fictional creature from *Arabian Nights* may be based on the huge, flightless elephant bird of Madagascar.

Hummingbird egg

Each egg weighs about one-fifth of the adult's weight.

Shell almost 2 mm thick

Ostrich egg

Each egg weighs up to 3.3 lb (1.5 kg)—about a hundredth of the adult's weight.

Hummingbirds

Hummingbirds come in various colors.

Tiny eggs

The smallest hummingbird eggs measure 0.4 in (1 cm) from end to end and weigh about 0.01 oz (0.35 g). The female lays only two eggs in the tiny nest.

Ostrich

Clubbing together

The ostrich lays the largest egg of any bird alive today. These birds often lay their eggs in the same place, creating a pile of up to 50 eggs.

Emu egg

An emu egg weighs just over one-hundredth of the adult's weight.

Kiwi egg

The egg is nearly one-quarter of the adult's weight.

Emu

Green to black

The eggs of the Australian emu are a dull green color when laid. Within a few days, they turn black and glossy.

Kiwi

Outsize egg

The kiwi lays the largest egg in proportion to her body of any bird. Each egg weighs about 1 lb (450 g) and takes two-and-a-half months to be incubated.

The volume of the elephant bird's egg is more than twice that of any dinosaur's egg.

Elephant bird egg

Elephant bird eggs weighed approximately 26 lb (12 kg) each—about 3 percent of the adult's body weight—making them among the largest eggs ever laid. Elephant birds lived in Madagascar, and although they died out about 700 years ago, whole eggs have been uncovered in the island's swamps.

Hatching

The shell of an egg is extremely strong, and a hatching bird spends hours or even days breaking this barrier to the outside world. Some nestlings are helpless and dependent on their parents for food. Others, such as the duckling shown here, are more developed and can fend for themselves within a few days of being born.

Week 1

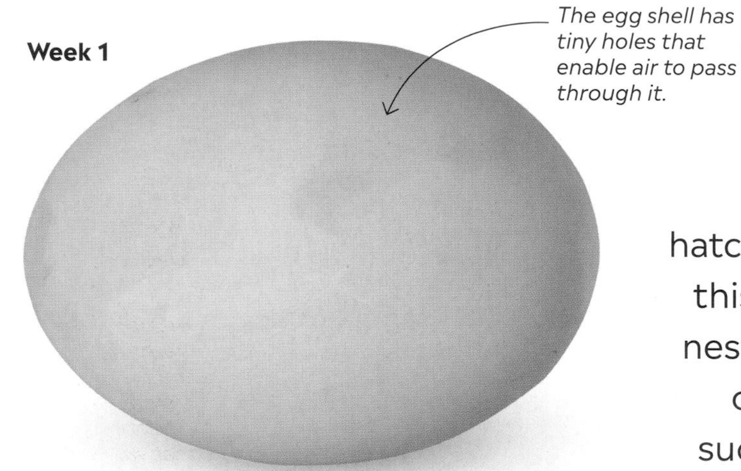

1 Developing embryo

The yolk and other nutritious fluids in the duck egg nourish the embryo. Within one week, the embryo grows, and the different organs and tissues are formed. By the second week, the eyes of the embryo are visible.

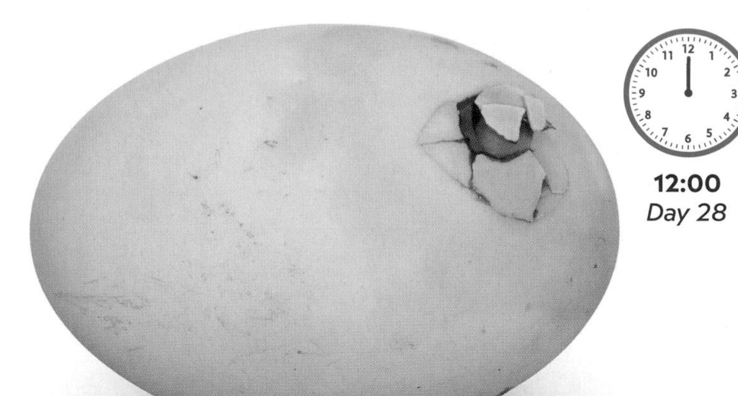

12:00
Day 28

2 Breaking the shell

After 28 days, the duck chick, still enclosed in the shell, turns around to point its beak toward the egg's blunt end. It breaks through the shell with the help of a special "egg tooth"—a sharp projection on its beak.

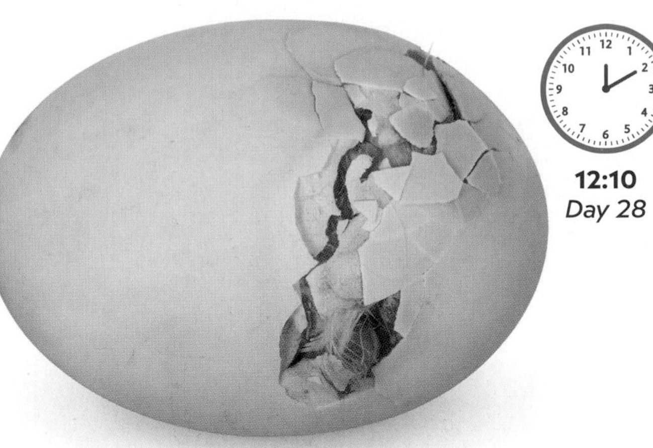

12:10
Day 28

3 Cutting a circle

The chick repeatedly pecks and turns inside the egg. It pushes with its feet to produce a crack that runs around the base of the egg's blunt end.

INSIDE THE EGG

Development of the embryo starts as soon as incubation begins. The shell and protective membranes protect the embryo.

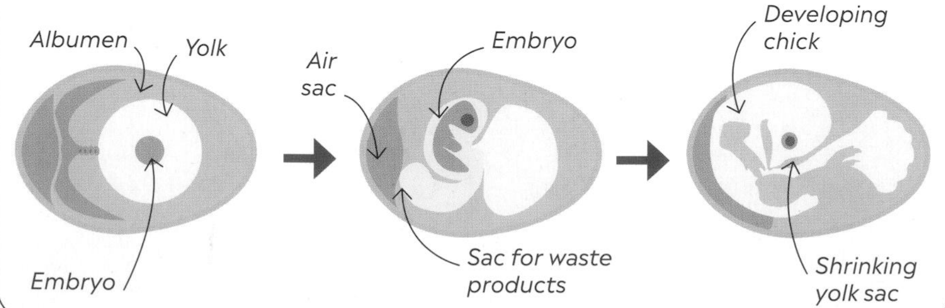

Newborn duckling

12:12
Day 28

4 Completing the circle

The chick has almost detached the blunt end from the rest of the egg. Large pieces of shell fall away as the chick continues to push.

5 Into the outside world

With a final push, the chick tumbles out of the shell. Before pushing, it moves its body and wriggles out of the membranes that have surrounded it.

Pheasant chicks are able to **fly two weeks after hatching.**

EYEWITNESS

Simon Griffith
British biologist Simon Griffith has analyzed the effects of climate change on plants and animals. His work has revealed that the warmer climate is making birds hatch early. It is also affecting nestlings that grow during summers in hot regions. They are developing into smaller adults.

12:20
Day 28

Within hours, its feathers will dry and fluff up to provide an insulating jacket that will keep it warm.

Growing **up**

Birds that are helpless after hatching, such as blue tits, usually grow at an extremely fast rate, fueled by a constant supply of food from their parents. Many studies of wild birds monitor nests in boxes, such as this brood of blue tits. Photos like these are taken by specially trained scientists who ensure the welfare of the birds.

EYEWITNESS

Julia Schroeder
Researcher Julia Schroeder studies the behavior of birds across generations on Lundy Island, UK. Each year, she monitors different birds including hundreds of sparrow chicks in nest boxes and has discovered that noise pollution is harming young sparrows.

Leg

Wing

Joined eyelids

1 One day old
Twenty-four hours after hatching, blue tit nestlings have no feathers, and their eyes are closed. Their parents bring food to the nest every few minutes.

Mouth brightly colored to attract attention

Feather tufts

2 Three days old
Small tufts of feathers have appeared, and the nestlings are about four times heavier than when they hatched.

Feather tract

Feather sheaths

3 Five days old
Dark gray feather tracts have appeared on the backs and wings. These areas will produce the birds' feathers.

A wren may make 1,000 trips a day to feed its chicks.

Feather sheaths

Emerging feather tips

Escape from danger

Although most birds protect their nestlings by bluff or aggression when threatened, some parents can pick up their young and carry them away. Depending on the species, they may use either their beak, legs, or talons to do this.

Water rail
The water rail carries its chicks in its beak.

Airlift
When startled, the woodcock will sometimes carry a chick between its legs to move it away from danger.

4 Nine days old

The feather tips have begun to emerge. Growing feathers are starting to cover the skin between the feather tracts.

These young birds will gradually learn how to look after themselves.

5 Thirteen days old

The nestlings are fully fledged, and their eyes are open. Within five days, they will leave the nest.

Attracting **birds**

The best way to attract birds into a garden is to provide a regular supply of food and give them a place to stay by placing nest boxes beyond the reach of cats. Seeds, nuts, kitchen scraps, and water will help birds survive cold winters. Studies suggest that feeding has caused a boom in the populations of some bird species. This may have led to an increase in competition for resources between different woodland birds.

St. Francis

St. Francis of Assisi is said to have had a special attraction for birds.

Hole-fronted

This straightforward design attracts tits and nuthatches.

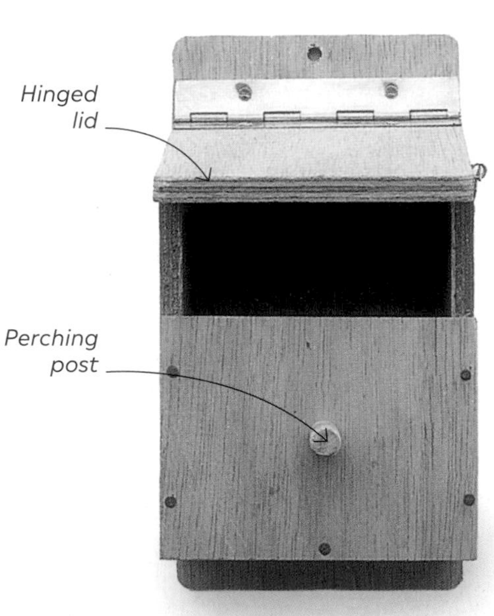

Open-fronted

This box needs to be well concealed to protect incubating birds.

Tits are attracted by nuts and fat on bird tables.

Removable lid for inspecting nest

Log boxes

A hollowed-out log makes an excellent home for small woodland birds.

Two halves of a log hollowed out and nailed together

Fancy boxes

A bird box with unnecessary ornaments may deter birds. Check that the box is sturdy and the roof is watertight.

Feeding table may attract other birds, disturbing those nesting in the box.

Mealworms

Insect-eating birds find these beetle grubs irresistible.

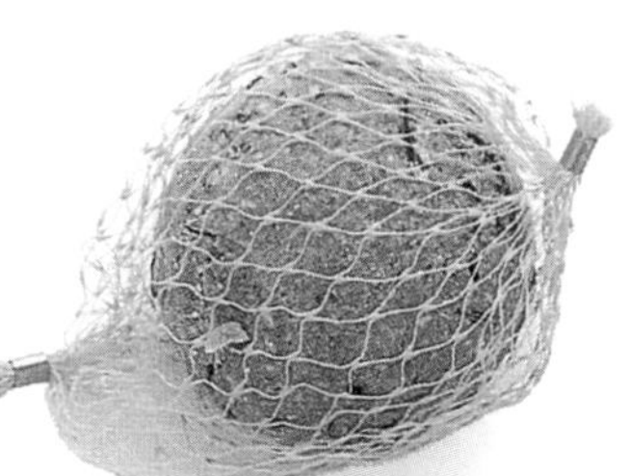

Fat and seed ball

Commercial "bird pudding"

Great spotted woodpecker feeding on peanuts

Acrobatic blue tits enjoy fresh coconut.

Seed cakes

Oils and fats are a rich source of energy for garden birds. Loose seeds can be pressed together with oil or fat to make a solid lump.

Loose seed

Mixtures of loose seed contain nutritious oil and fats.

Bread

Brown bread makes a far better bird food than white.

Hunger sometimes forces birds to become particularly tame in winter.

Seed dispenser

Thistle seeds are popular with such birds as the house finch, American goldfinch, and indigo bunting. Bird feeders should be cleaned at least once a month.

Niger seeds

Perching post

In the open

Open habitats, such as coastal areas, are ideal locations to observe distant birds by using binoculars and telescopes without frightening them away. It is important to avoid disturbing birds while watching them.

Watching **birds**

An experienced birdwatcher can recognize different bird species as a result of careful observation—looking at the shape and color of birds, watching the way they live or fly, or even listening to their songs.

Keeping a notebook

A field guide is essential to identify birds, but noting behavior and making sketches will also help build your knowledge.

Sketching

Use colored pencils to sketch details instead of writing lengthy notes.

Ruler for measuring feathers

EYEWITNESS

Mya-Rose Craig

The 21-year-old British-Bangladeshi naturalist Mya-Rose Craig has traveled around the world and managed to see more than half of the known species of birds. She has also written a book—*Birdgirl: Looking to the Skies in Search of a Better Future*—where she recounts her birdwatching experiences.

Buzzard feather

Pigeon feathers

Shearwater feather

Storing feathers

Store feathers in bags to prevent damage.

Examining pellets

Many of the animal remains inside bird pellets are very delicate and can be damaged when a pellet is pulled apart. If you use a magnifying glass and a pair of tweezers, small bones and teeth can be separated without breaking.

Portable telescope

Magnifying glass

Plastic tweezers are less likely to damage bones than metal ones.

Photography

Taking pictures of wild birds—especially in flight—is difficult. Practice using your camera with garden birds before venturing farther afield. A telephoto lens allows you to zoom in closer to your subject without causing a disturbance.

200 mm telephoto lens

Using binoculars

For serious birdwatching, you will need a pair of binoculars. They should be lightweight and have good magnification plus a fairly wide field of view.

Eyepiece lens

Tripod

Cameras that use high power lenses need a steady support to keep the image blurring. A lightweight tripod is essential. It can also be used for mounting binoculars.

Did you **know?**

FASCINATING FACTS

There are more than 10,980 species of birds in the world. About two-thirds of all bird species are found in tropical rain forests.

Hoatzin

Hoatzin chicks have two claws on each wing. Once the birds have grown, they lose their claws, but they are not good fliers.

Owls cannot swivel their eyes. Instead they turn their heads right around to see behind them.

Kiwis are unique in having nostrils right at the end of their beaks so they can sniff for food on the ground.

Brown kiwi

Instead of singing, a woodpecker drums its beak against a tree.

The most talkative bird in the world is the African gray parrot. One bird was such a good mimic that it could say 800 words.

The marsh warbler is a talented mimic. It has been recorded mimicking the calls of more than 80 different birds.

The secretary bird kills snakes by stamping on them. It uses its wings as a shield to protect itself from being bitten.

Secretary bird eating a snake

The pelican's huge, pouchlike beak can hold up to 2.2 gallons (10 litres) of water at a time.

The lammergeier, a vulture, carries bones high into the air, then drops them onto rocks. It then eats the smashed bones, taking them into its mouth.

Instead of making a nest, the mallee fowl builds a huge compost heap in which the female lays her eggs. The eggs are incubated in the heat given off by the rotting vegetation.

Social weaver birds live in a huge communal nest like a haystack spread across a treetop. The nest may be 100 years old, weigh a few tons, and have 400 birds living in it.

The condor's giant wings are used for gliding.

Condor

The Andean condor is the heaviest bird of prey, weighing up to 26.4 lb (12 kg).

The shimmering colors on the tail feathers of the male peacock are actually an impression caused by micro structures that reflect light.

No sooner has the Count Raggi's bird of paradise mated with one female than it starts displaying again to win the attention of another.

Raggiana bird of paradise

QUESTIONS AND ANSWERS

What is the most common wild bird in the world?

The red-billed quelea is the world's most numerous wild bird. More than 1.5 billion of them live in Africa.

Peregrine

Which bird can fly the fastest?

When a peregrine falcon swoops down on its prey, it can reach speeds of over 110 mph (180 kmph), making it the fastest-flying bird.

How long do birds live, and which bird lives the longest?

Songbirds may live between 8 and 12 years, while hummingbirds live for 6 to 8 years, and warblers 3 to 6 years. Some birds, such as penguins and albatrosses, live longer. The large Laysan albatross can live for up to 80 years.

Which birds are best at swimming?

Gentoo penguins are the fastest swimmers, reaching speeds of 22.3 mph (36 kmph). Emperor penguins can stay underwater for up to 18 minutes.

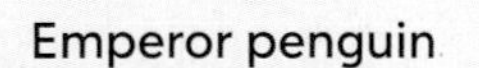

Emperor penguin

Penguins use their small, stiff wings like flippers to propel them through the water.

Which birds spend the most time in the air?

Swifts spend most of their lives in the air. They even sleep in flight, gliding on air currents with their wings outstretched.

Which bird makes the longest journey when migrating?

Arctic terns make one of the longest annual migrations of any bird. They fly 25,000 miles (40,000 km) from the Arctic to the Antarctic and then back again.

How do migrating birds find their way across the world?

Migrating birds follow the same routes every year, but nobody knows exactly how. They may use the position of the sun and stars to help them find their way, or they may follow prominent features in the landscape below them, such as coastlines and mountains. Some people think that they might also use Earth's magnetic field.

Wandering albatross

Wingspan of up to 11.9 ft (3.63 m)

Why do some birds have huge wings?

The wandering albatross has the greatest wingspan of any bird. It spends most of its life above the ocean, using its huge wings to soar in light winds.

How high in the sky can birds fly?

Bar-headed geese fly across the Himalayan mountains when migrating to their winter feeding grounds in India. They fly at heights of nearly 5 miles (more than 8,000 m)—almost as high as jet planes.

RECORD BREAKERS

Biggest bird
The ostrich is the largest, tallest, and heaviest bird. Male ostriches are up to 9 ft (2.7 m) tall.

Smallest bird
The bee hummingbird of Cuba is the smallest bird in the world. It is 2.2 in (5.7 cm) long, and its beak and tail cover about half its size.

Fastest level flight
The spine-tailed swift and the red-breasted merganser have been credited with flying at 100 mph (161 kmph) in level flight.

Wing-beat speed
During courtship display, the ruby-throated hummingbird can beat its wings at a rate of 200 beats per second.

Identifying **birds**

To make identification easier, birds are divided into different groups, based on characteristics that they share. The biggest group of birds is the passerines (sparrow-shaped birds), which include the perching and singing birds.

BIRD GROUPS

Flightless birds
This group contains species that run but cannot fly. On land, they include ostriches, rheas, cassowaries, and kiwis.

Ostrich

Strong legs for fast running

Long, shaggy wing feathers

Short, thick toes

Rhea

Wading birds
Many birds, such as spoonbills, flamingos, and herons, wade into water to find food. Most have long legs and probing beaks to catch fish and crustaceans.

Roseate spoonbill

Spoon-shaped bill sweeps sideways through water.

Juvenile greater flamingo

Stiltlike legs

Dagger-shaped bill

Black-crowned night heron

Waterfowl
Swans, geese, and ducks are waterfowl and live near rivers, ponds, and lakes. They have webbed feet and large beaks.

Long, flexible neck

Mute swan

Stocky build and upright stance

Swan goose

Common shelduck

Some ducks may have bold markings.

BIRD GROUPS

Birds of prey
Meat-eating hunters, such as kestrels, eagles, and owls, have excellent eyesight and long legs with talons for catching prey. They use their strong, hooked beaks to tear prey apart. Owls are usually nocturnal. These silent predators have excellent night vision, hooked beaks, and sharp talons.

Shorebirds
This large group includes gulls, terns, puffins, and guillemots. They live on coasts, marshland, and mud flats.

Parrots
This group includes colorful, noisy birds, such as parrots, lorikeets, cockatoos, and macaws.

Game birds
Pheasants, partridges, and quails are all game birds. They spend most of the time on the ground but take to the air when in danger.

Kingfishers and hoopoes
Most of the birds in this group have brightly colored plumage and large beaks. They eat insects and sometimes reptiles and small mammals.

Passerines
This group contains over half of all bird species, including swallows, thrushes, warblers, tits, and crows.

Nuts and seeds attract blue tits to a garden.

Blue tits

Bright blue color on the head and wings

Find out **more**

You can learn a lot about birds by observing those in the area around your home, but to see different varieties, you will need to visit different habitats. Going for a walk in the country or by the water can introduce you to many interesting new species. You could also visit bird reserves, sanctuaries, or national parks to see more rare and unusual birds.

Parks and gardens

Parks and gardens are good places to observe birds. With their trees, flowerbeds, and ponds, they provide a wealth of different habitats.

Swans at a wildfowl and wetlands center

Wetlands

Lakes, rivers, swamps, and marshes are home to a wide variety of birds, from swans and ducks to herons and storks. Here, food is plentiful, and there are safe nesting places in reeds and on the banks.

National parks

From high mountains to deep lakes, complex cave systems to dry deserts, national parks contain different landscapes. Some bird species can be found only in these protected habitats.

Ostriches in Tarangire National Park, South Africa

PLACES TO VISIT

YELLOWSTONE NATIONAL PARK, WYOMING
• A wide range of birds can be found at the different elevations within the park.

FLORIDA EVERGLADES, FLORIDA
• The greater flamingo and coastal birds, including short-tailed hawks, great blue herons, and bald eagles live here.

JAMAICA BAY WILDLIFE REFUGE, NEW YORK CITY
• More than 330 species have been seen in this Queens park, a popular stop along many migration routes.

USEFUL WEBSITES

- The National Audobon Society works to protect birds and their natural habitats: **www.audubon.org**
- Wild Bird Centers of America provides extensive information about feeding birds in your own backyard: **www.birdfeeding.org**
- CornellLab Merlin is an app which helps bird watchers identify birds. It can be used in any country of the world: **merlin.allaboutbirds.org**

Crimson rosella

Tropical forests

When on vacation, it is well worth visiting national parks to see native species of birds. The Lamington National Park in Queensland, Australia, is home to many tropical birds.

Coastlines

The coast is a good place to see gulls and other seabirds. Look out for waders feeding on worms and shellfish in the shallow waters of estuaries.

Gannet colony

Golden-fronted woodpecker

Forest and woodland

With plenty of nuts, seeds, and insects to eat and safe places to nest, forests and woodlands provide a rich habitat for birds.

IDENTIFYING BIRDS BY THEIR FLIGHT SILHOUETTE

Look out for these flight silhouettes to help you identify the birds you see.

Narrow, tapering wings
Fast-fliers, such as swallows and swifts, have slender wings and forked tails.

Swallow

Long, elegant wings
Seabirds that spend a lot of time in the air have long, narrow wings.

Tern

Broad, pointed wings
Falcons have narrow tails and broad, pointed wings for high-speed flying.

Falcon

Massive wingspan
Long-distance gliders have long, pointed wings to glide on warm currents of air. It is quite rare to spot an albatross.

Albatross

Feathered fingers
Eagles and vultures have large, wide wings with splayed "fingers."

Eagle

Short, round wings
Many woodland birds have short, wide, rounded wings to fly among trees.

Sparrowhawk

Glossary

A gannet colony

ALULA A group of feathers on the leading edge of a bird's wing that prevents it from stalling as it slows down.

BARBS Tiny side branches off a feather shaft that make up a bird's feather.

BINOCULAR VISION The area of sight in which the fields of vision of both eyes overlap. Binocular vision enables birds to judge distances accurately.

BLIND A structure or small building where people can hide to watch birds without disturbing them.

BODY FEATHERS (OR CONTOUR) The small, overlapping feathers on a bird's head and body that give it a streamlined shape.

BREED To find a partner, mate, build a nest, lay eggs, and raise chicks.

BREEDING SEASON The time of year when birds mate, build nests, lay eggs, and raise their chicks.

CAMOUFLAGE The color and patterning of a bird's feathers and eggs that match its surroundings and make it hard to see.

Body feather

CLUTCH The total number of eggs that is incubated by a parent bird or a pair of birds at any one time.

COLONY A large group of birds that live together in one place to breed or roost, or the place in which they live.

Clutch of eggs

COURTSHIP The behavior of birds when finding partners before mating. It may take the form of special movements, dancing, or songs.

COVERTS Groups of small feathers that cover the base of the main flight feathers.

DABBLING The way a duck feeds, by opening and shutting its beak while skimming it across the surface of the water.

DISPLAY A conspicuous pattern of movements and colorful plumage used to communicate with other birds of the same species, especially in courtship or when threatened.

DISTRIBUTION All the areas in which a bird is seen regularly.

DOWN FEATHERS Very soft, fine feathers that trap air close to a bird's body and help keep it warm.

EGG TOOTH A small structure on the tip of a chick's upper bill, which it uses to crack open the eggshell when hatching. The egg tooth drops off soon after hatching.

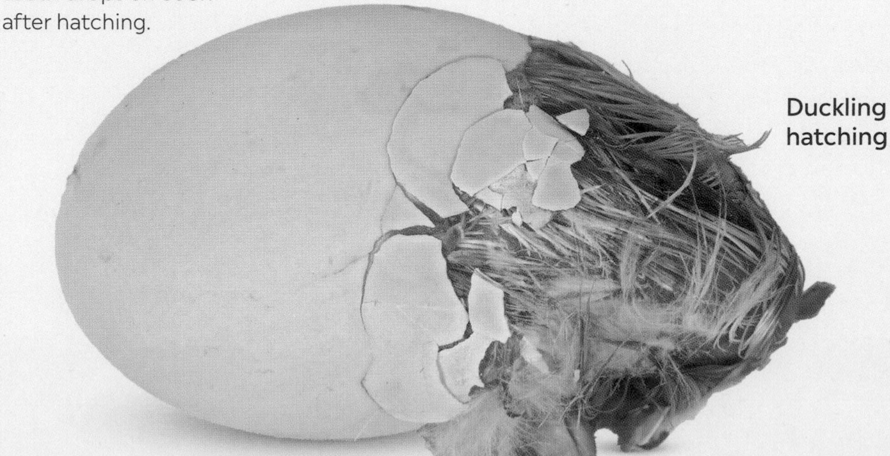

Duckling hatching

EXTINCTION The process by which living things, such as the dodo, die out completely and no longer exist.

FIELD GUIDE A pocket-sized book that helps the reader identify different birds.

FLEDGE To leave the nest.

FLIGHT FEATHERS The long feathers that make up a bird's wings and are used to fly. They can be grouped into primary feathers (on the outer wing) and secondary feathers (on the inner wing).

Blue tit nestlings

FLOCK A group of birds flying or feeding together.

GIZZARD The muscular chamber in a bird's stomach, where food material is ground up into a pulp.

HABITAT The type of environment where a bird is normally found, such as wetland, forest, or grassland.

Blind at a bird reserve

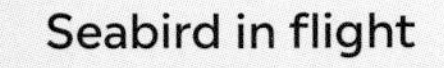

Seabird in flight

HATCHING The process by which a baby bird breaks out of its egg by chipping its way through the shell with the tiny egg tooth on its beak.

INCUBATION Providing constant warmth for eggs so that chicks can develop inside them. Most birds incubate their eggs by sitting on them to keep them warm.

INVERTEBRATE A type of small animal that has no backbone, such as a worm.

IRIDESCENT The glittering sheen on some feathers and other objects that appears to change color, depending on the direction of the light.

KEEL A large, platelike extension of a flying bird's breastbone, which anchors its powerful wing muscles in place.

KERATIN A type of protein from which feathers, hair, nails, and hooves are made.

MANDIBLE One of the two parts of a bird's beak (bill). The upper mandible is the top part, and the lower mandible is the bottom part.

MIGRATE To travel from one place to another regularly in search of a plentiful food supply or good breeding grounds.

MOLTING Shedding worn-out feathers and growing new ones in their place.

MONOCULAR VISION The area seen by one eye only rather than by both eyes working together.

NECTAR The sweet liquid produced by a flower to attract birds and insects to feed from the flower and pollinate it.

NESTLING A baby bird that is still in the nest and cannot fly.

NOCTURNAL Active by night.

ORNITHOLOGIST A person who studies birds.

PELLET A hard lump of indigestible bits of food, such as fur and bones, that birds regurgitate.

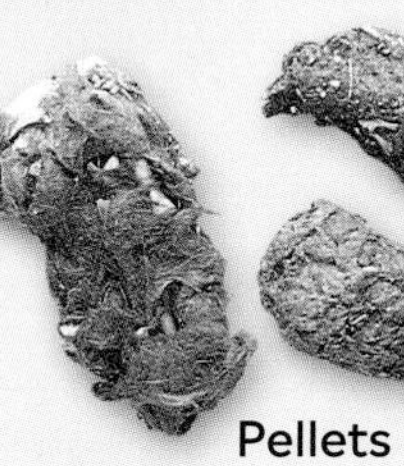

Pellets

PLUMAGE A bird's feathers.

POWDER DOWN Special feathers on some birds that disintegrate to form a powder, which the bird uses to clean its plumage.

PREDATOR An animal that kills another animal for food.

PREENING The way in which birds keep their feathers in good condition, drawing them through their beaks to clean them.

PREY An animal that is hunted and killed by another animal.

PRIMARY FEATHERS The long flight feathers on the outer half of the wings, used for steering and turning.

QUILL The long, hollow central shaft of a bird's feather.

REGURGITATE To bring food that has been swallowed back up into the mouth again, often to feed the young.

ROOST To settle down to rest, normally overnight.

SCAVENGER A bird, such as a vulture, that searches for dead animals to eat.

Flight feather

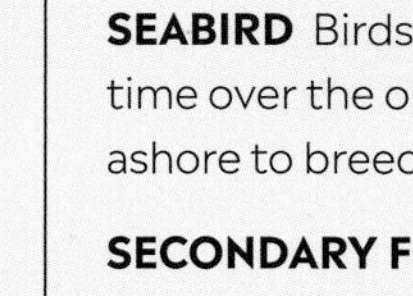

SEABIRD Birds that spend most of their time over the open sea and only come ashore to breed.

SECONDARY FEATHERS One of the inner wing feathers.

SPECIES A group of birds of the same type that can breed with one another and live in the same area.

SPECULUM A white or colored patch that some ducks have across the inner wing feathers.

STOOP To swoop down (bird of prey).

TALONS The sharp, curved claws of a bird of prey.

TERRITORY An area occupied by a bird that it may defend against other birds of the same species.

TERTIALS A bird's innermost flight feathers, which shape the wing to the body to ensure a smooth flight.

Red-breasted goose preening its feathers

THERMAL A rising column of warm air, often at the edge of a cliff or hillside, on which soaring birds glide.

VERTEBRATE Any animal that has a backbone. Birds are vertebrates.

WILDFOWL A wide range of mostly web-footed birds found in, on, or near water, such as ducks, geese and swans.

Index

Acknowledgments

The publisher would like to thank the following people for their help with making the book: Phyilip Amies; the staff of the Natural History Department, City of Bristol Museum; the staff of the British Museum Natural History at Tring; Martin Brown of the Wildfowl Trust, Slimbridge, & Rosemary Crawford for their advice & invaluable help in providing specimens; Steve Parker & Anne-Marie Bulat for their work on the initial stages of the book; Fred Ford & Mike Pilley of Radius Graphics, & Ray Owen & Nick Madren for artwork; Tanvi Sahu and Adarsh Tripathi for design assistance; Tim Hammond and Aman Kumar for editoral assistance; Hazel Beynon for proofreading; and Elizabeth Wise for the index.

Publisher's note: No bird has been injured or in any way harmed during the preparation of this book.

For the previous edition, the publisher would also like to thank: the author for assisting with revisions; Claire Bowers, David Ekholm-JAlbum, Sunita Gahir, Joanne Little, Nigel Ritchie, Susan St Louis, Carey Scott, & Bulent Yusuf for the clipart; David Ball, Neville Graham, Rose Horridge, Joanne Little, & Sue Nicholson for the wallchart; BCP, Marianne Petrou, & Owen Peyton Jones for checking the digitized files.

The publisher would like to thank the following for their kind permission to reproduce their images:
(a=above, b=below/bottom, c=centre, f=far, l=left, r=right, t=top)

Alamy Stock Photo: All Canada Photos / Glen Bartley 16cl (cb), Associated Press / Anupam Nath 47tr, Avalon. red / John Shaw 69tc, blickwinkel / Carrasco 32tc, blickwinkel / fotototo 20c, Cathy & Gordon Illg / Jaynes Gallery / DanitaDelimont.com 68bl, Andrew Darrington 32tr, David Tipling Photo Library 62-63t, Daybreak Imagery 61r, Eureka 56crb, Peter J. Hatcher 60tr, Denis-Huot Michel / Hemis.fr 21r, Dozier Marc / Hemis.fr 64br, David Hosking 49bc, Imagebroker / Arco / G. Lacz 2c, imageBROKER.com GmbH & Co. KG / Winfried Schfer 46tl, Len Collection 23cra, Alan Murphy / BIA / Minden Pictures 10tl, D. Parer & E. Parer-Cook / Minden Pictures 28bl, Douglas Herr / BIA / Minden Pictures 19cra, Konrad Wothe / Minden Pictures 8-9c, Natural History Museum, London 6tl, Nature Photographers Ltd / PAUL R. STERRY 51bl, Nature Picture Library / Alan Williams 68cr, Nature Picture Library / Bence Mate 40cra, Nature Picture Library / Colin Varndell 12cl, Nature Picture Library / Connor Stefanison 15crb, Nature Picture Library / Kim Taylor 4tl, 13tl, 32bc, Nature Picture Library / Sergey Gorshkov 18-19b, Nature Picture Library / Wild Wonders of Europe / Varesvu 12cb, North Wind Picture Archives 10bc, Our Wild Life Photography 19crb, Panther Media GmbH / Kiefer 17bc, Kumud Parajuli 48l, Premium Stock Photography GmbH / Willi Rolfes 16-17t, Prisma Archivo 10cl, Malcolm Schuyl 21bc, 64cla, Roger Harris / Science Photo Library 6clb, Sebastian 64ca, Graham Turner 63clb, Ian West 30cla, ZSSD / Minden Pictures 34bc; **Alex Bond:** 41tr; **Ardea London:** Tony & Liz Bomford 14mr; **Bridgeman Art Library:** 13tr; 28tr; 52t; 61b; **Bruce Coleman Ltd:** 64cl; Johnny Johnson 65bl; Gordon Langsbury 13b; 14b; Allan G. Ports 69tr; Robert Wilmshurst 15b; **Dorling Kindersley:** Andrew Beckett (Illustration Ltd) 36ca; **Dreamstime.com:** Stuart Andrews 12cr, Harry Collins 14cla, David Herraez 17crb, Karin59 67crb, Johannes Gerhardus Swanepoel 66cl; **Gabrielle Nevitt:** Terry ODwyer 35cra; **Getty Images:** 500px Prime / Gerhard Kummer 13cra, Geoff Caddick / AFP 62bc, imageBROKER / Friedhelm Adam 19tl, imageBROKER / Gilles Barbier 36-37c, Moment / Gary Mayes 28-29c, Moment Open / Jill Ferry 69cl, The Image Bank / Winfried Wisniewski 12bl; **Getty Images / iStock:** Adrian Coleman 19ca, pum_eva 13cb; **Gables:** 66-67bkg, 70-71bkg; **Simon Griffith:** 57cra; **Sonia Halliday:** 60tr. **Robert Harding:** Brian Hawkes 47t; **Frank Lane Picture Agency:** 12bl, 14m, 16t, 29t, ml, 33b, 35tr, 37mr, bl, tl, 46m, 47m, 60tl, m, 63; R. Austing 32 br; C. Carvalho 17t; J.K. Fawcett 12mr; T. & P. Gardner 21bl; John Hawkins 13tl; 19tl; 35m; Peggy Heard 61m; R. Jones 17m; Derek A. Robinson 8m, 47b; H. Schrempp 32bl; Roger Tidman 36tr; B.S. Turner 42t; R. Van Tidman 37br; John Watkins/ Tidman 33ml; Robert Wilmshurst/ Tidman 12 br; 46t; 49t; W. Wisniewski/ Tidman 37ml; J. Zimmermann/ Tidman 31tr; 36b; **Mansell Collection:** 6t, 10ml; 34t; 54; **Mary Evans Picture Library:** 6bl, br; 9tr, mr; 10t, mr, b; 20bl; 24t; 26t; 30mr; 32m; 36t, mr; 38t; 41t; 54tl, tr, bl; 56t; 58b; **naturepl.com:** Guy Edwardes 12bc, 37tc, Orsolya Haarberg 32bl, Andy Sands 36crb, Phil Savoie 29tc, Kim Taylor 13ca, Markus Varesvuo 34tr; **Natural History Museum:** 70cl, cr, bl, 71ca, bl; **NHPA:** Bruce Beehler 64br; G.I. Bernard 21ml, mr; Manfred Danegger 13m; Hellio & Van Ingen 40b; Michael Leach 34m; Crimson Rosella 69tl; Jonathan and Angela Scott 64c; Philip Wayre 19br; Alan Williams 68cr; **Oceanwidelmages.com:** Chris & Monique Fallows 40-41b; **Oxford Scientific Films:** Richard Herrmann 68bc; Ronald Toms 68tl; **Pickthall Library:** 15t; **Planet Earth Pictures:** A.P. Barnes 15m; **Press-Tige Pictures:** 12mr; **Julia Schroeder:** 58tr; **Science Photo Library:** Sinclair Stammers 6m, Dennis Kunkel Microscopy 20ca; **Shutterstock.com:** Bplanet 63br, Luka Hercigonja 63bl, Hitesh Jain 14-15t**South of England Rare Breed Centre:** 66crb; **Survival Anglia:** Jen & Des Bartlett 54br; Jeff Foott 31mr; **Alan Williams:** 71tl; **Jerry Young:** 66tl

All other images © Dorling Kindersley

DK WHAT WILL YOU EYEWITNESS NEXT?

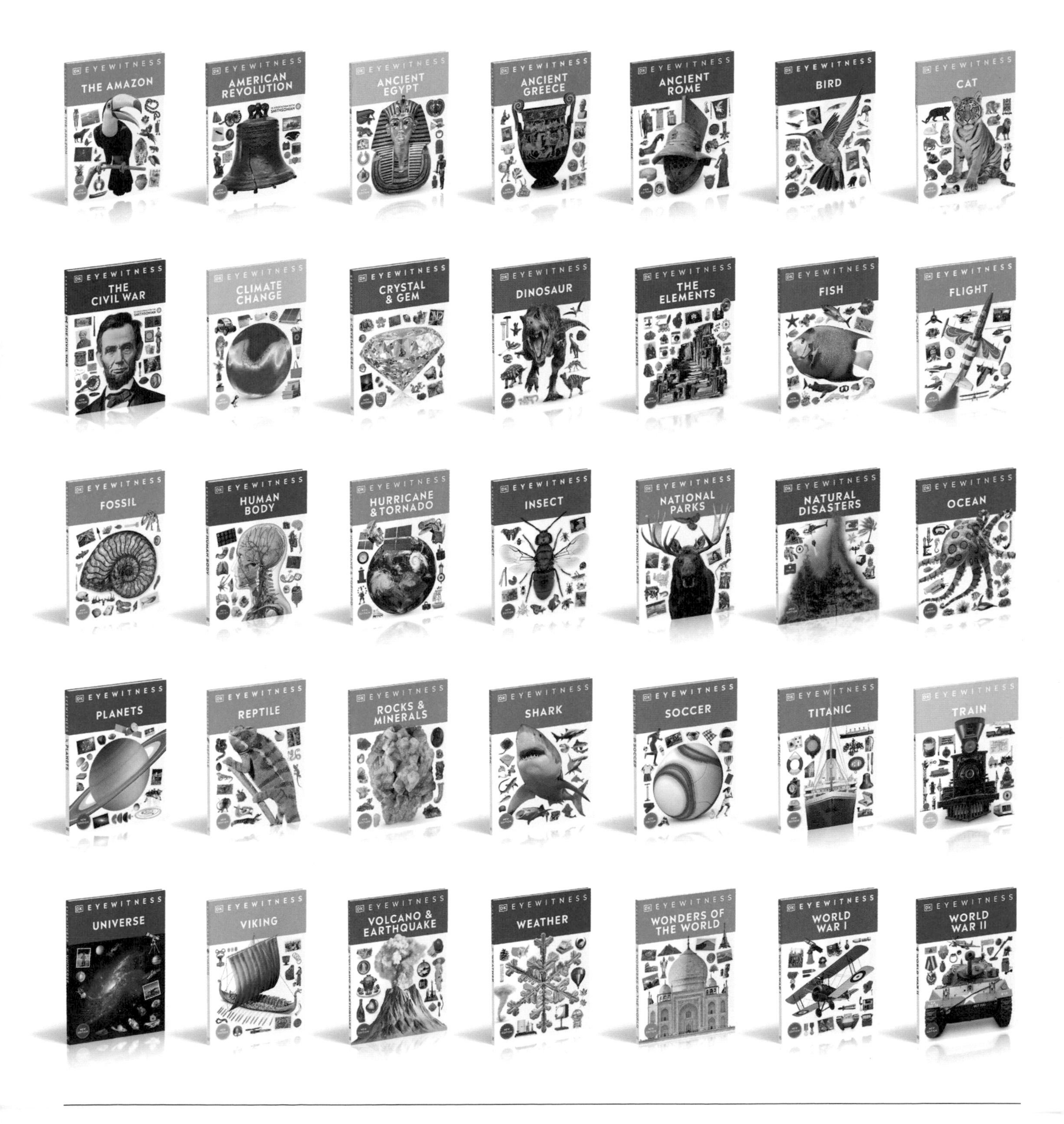

Also available:

Eyewitness Amphibian
Eyewitness Ancient China
Eyewitness Ancient Civilizations
Eyewitness Animal
Eyewitness Arms and Armor
Eyewitness Astronomy
Eyewitness Aztec, Inca & Maya
Eyewitness Baseball
Eyewitness Bible Lands
Eyewitness Car
Eyewitness Dog
Eyewitness Eagle and Birds of Prey
Eyewitness Electricity
Eyewitness Endangered Animals
Eyewitness Energy
Eyewitness Forensic Science
Eyewitness Great Scientists
Eyewitness Horse
Eyewitness Judaism
Eyewitness Knight
Eyewitness Medieval Life
Eyewitness Mesopotamia
Eyewitness Mythology
Eyewitness Plant
Eyewitness Prehistoric Life
Eyewitness Presidents
Eyewitness Religion
Eyewitness Robot
Eyewitness Shakespeare
Eyewitness Soldier
Eyewitness Space Exploration
Eyewitness Tree
Eyewitness Vietnam War